The Hupomone Principle

Finding Purpose and Freedom in Biblical Perseverance

Samuel R. Guidry

Table of Contents

Preface

The Hupomone Principle began first as a personal exploration of perseverance and then as a word study inspired by the Holy Spirit. Its first public expression was as a series of devotionals on a local Christian radio station, YES FM. As I explored this biblical concept, I realized how absent it was from the modern Christian mindset. Add to this that too many times when it was expressed it was s incorrectly applied as some onerous condition of the regenerate life that was somehow propped up by the Holy Spirit so that we could (just barely) endure the rigors that life on earth throws our way.

I encourage the reader to step out of this world's atmosphere of impermanence and its throw-away mentality into a place of eternal design where relationships last and we have a God who can be trusted to always be there, even when we can't sense Him. It is a place where we walk through storms and can hold on to the joy of the Lord, not in a foolish effervescent way but with a deep conviction that God is guiding our steps and guarding our path.

The Hupomone Principle has taken shape with the input of so many, both brothers and sisters in Christ and people who have impacted us without our faith in their lives, people I continue to pray for. It spans a lifetime of running both away from Jesus Christ and to Him. This is a simple introduction to a life principle that will give you purpose and freedom in your walk with God. If you do not have a relationship with Jesus Christ, I pray that The Hupomone Principle inspires you to pursue Him because He is pursuing you.

Even as I put the finishing touches on The Hupomone Principle I am working on The Journey to Hupomone which will explore in more detail my personal experience finding biblical perseverance. Perhaps by putting myself on the line here I will finish this project in less than the six years The Hupomone Principle took to complete.

Just as a side note, as I get ready to release this book, I am now employed by the radio station where it publicly started, God's sense of timing, humor and Hupomone in action.

Samuel Guidry
November 2020

Chapter 1

Introduction to Hupomone

*Now may the God who gives perseverance and
encouragement grant you to be
of the same mind with one another according to Christ
Jesus.*

—Romans 15:5

Beginnings

I had not thought much about endurance in my first 40 years of life. It was a topic that was meant more for certain sports or for those living through persecution or suffering. Endurance or perseverance was a function of circumstances in my life and not a spiritual value. One could simply avoid the need to endure or persevere by avoiding negative circumstances. I applied the concept more to sitting through boring church services and business meetings than to my day-to-day living.

The roller-coaster life that ensued was destructive to me and to those near me. I structured my life to avoid boredom and to avoid the need for perseverance altogether. The result was a failed marriage and a complete lack of active faith where I perceived the distance between God and me to be insurmountable. When the circumstances of life made me a single dad of two, I realized that something had to change. I did what I always did and battled circumstances with circumstances. I started attending a local church. I stopped drinking and curtailed my social life. While these were all good things to do, they did not address the spiritual desert I was living in.

It took me a few years to begin the long learning process that God had before me—to discover the nature of a godly man. He brought into my life a woman—Allana—who was walking a similar road, and we began to grow together in the Holy Spirit. Still, we moved from job to job and from ministry to ministry as I got bored. But now, it was not just about getting bored or looking for the next adrenalin fix. Each new venture brought spiritual lessons and growth in my relationship with God. He brought me in proximity to some great men of God while also walking with me and Allana through the fires of life's difficulties. He carefully allowed us to grow and be shaped by the Holy Spirit until we answered His call in 2009 to focus on serving Him as our full-time vocation and relying on Him for the plan and purpose of our lives. We soaked up this new lifestyle and found spiritual guidance in the most unusual places.

In 2013, Allana was diagnosed with leukemia. It was 19 days after our youngest daughter, Nisa Faith, was born. We agonized about how to tell our other children—my two boys, John and Robert; Allana's daughter, Samantha, who I had adopted; and our nine-year-old daughter, Chayla, our family-blender. Then, early in 2014, God impressed on me the word *hupomone* as I was studying his Word in Romans 5 and soaking in His Spirit. After a year of walking with Allana through the treatment protocols for acute lymphoblastic leukemia, it seemed like an appropriate topic. After all, the key verses about perseverance that we all know are found in Romans 5.

> *Therefore, having been justified by faith, we have peace with God through our Lord Jesus Christ, through whom also we have obtained our introduction by faith into this grace in which we stand; and we exult in hope of the glory of God. And not only this, but we also exult in our tribulations, knowing that tribulation brings about perseverance; and perseverance, proven character; and proven character, hope; and hope does not disappoint, because the love of God has been poured out within our hearts through the Holy Spirit who was given to us.*

—Rom. 5:1–5

Unfortunately, it seems that too often an exploration of perseverance stops with the idea of suffering, and then perseverance and suffering are forever linked as cause and effect. This important quality of life in Christ deserves a closer look. The Bible has a lot to say about perseverance. The word most often translated as perseverance,

endurance, or steadfastness is the Greek word *hupomone.*
As with so many Greek words (and English, too, I might
add), it is a combination of two root words: *upo* and *meno.*

> *upo:* about, under

> *meno:* abide, remain, stay, continue to be, survive,
> held or kept continually

Breaking it down and putting it back together again brings
us to this idea of remaining under or about something.
Often, it seems this idea is taken to mean remaining under
the problems and trials that life brings. When asked about a
trial going on in one's life, the easy answer seems to be,
"We are persevering!" We may not use that word much
anymore, but when we distill all the answers we give and
all the advice that comes in, it comes down to abiding
under the trial until it ends. The problem with this view of
perseverance is that it is focused on the trial, the trouble,
or the problem, not on our amazing God who is the
ultimate solution. Hupomone is not about super-moaning
through life as we bounce from trial to trial. Biblical
perseverance encompasses Romans 8:37: "But in all these
things we overwhelmingly conquer through Him who loved
us."

The source of perseverance tells us a lot about its
characteristics. The epigraph at the beginning of this
chapter makes it clear where perseverance comes from:

> *Now may the God who gives perseverance.*

Biblical perseverance is first and foremost a gift from God. It is one of those gifts that Jesus was talking about in Matthew 7:11:

> *If you then, being evil, know how to give good gifts to your children, how much more will your Father who is in heaven give what is good to those who ask Him!*

Love

> *And He said to him, "'YOU SHALL LOVE THE LORD YOUR GOD WITH ALL YOUR HEART, AND WITH ALL YOUR SOUL, AND WITH ALL YOUR MIND.' This is the great and foremost commandment. The second is like it, 'YOU SHALL LOVE YOUR NEIGHBOR AS YOURSELF.' On these two commandments depend the whole Law and the Prophets."*

—Matt. 22:37–40

This spiritual gift from God has many aspects. Love is one of them. The title of this section—Love—might indicate that it is a discussion of our need to continue in love even when those around us make it exceedingly difficult. There could perhaps be an enumeration of all the ways those both near and distant make it hard for us to love them. I am certain that I could easily come up with a list of ways I make it difficult to be loved. However, this is not the case. We are looking at love as a prime characteristic of perseverance.

It was established in the first part of this chapter that biblical perseverance is a gift from God, not something we work at, struggle for, or achieve through our own efforts. That does not relieve us of the responsibility of opening and exercising this gift. We just need to understand its source. Remaining under Jesus regardless of our circumstances (good and bad) is something that Paul understood. Consider his statement to the Philippians.

> *Not that I speak from want, for I have learned to be content in whatever circumstances I am.*

> —Phil. 4:11

He also understood the centrality of love to the very existence of God's children, expressing it wonderfully in 1 Corinthians 13. It should be no surprise that we find love at the center of biblical perseverance and that we have perseverance at the heart of biblical love. The salvation story, extending from Adam to Jesus to the first-century church and beyond, is a wonderful statement of this idea. It expresses love without regard to circumstances, appearances, or reciprocation.

> *But God demonstrates His own love toward us, in that while we were yet sinners, Christ died for us.*

> —Rom. 5:8

Paul directly links the nature of God's love and perseverance in 2 Thessalonians 3:5: "May the Lord direct your hearts into the love of God and into the steadfastness of Christ." *Hupomone* here is translated *steadfastness*.

The love of God is supremely expressed in the steadfastness of Christ and the course of action He undertook to be our salvation.

> *Being found in appearance as a man, He humbled Himself by becoming obedient to the point of death, even death on a cross.*

—Phil. 2:8

We have seen that hupomone is not something we slog through on our own. It is not groaning continually as we hold the course through difficult times. It is a gift from God. Biblical perseverance is at its core; God allows us to partake in His divine nature and all that means. As such, it brings with it all the fruit of the Spirit so that, with Paul, we can be "content in whatever circumstances" (Phil. 4:11) we find ourselves in. It is the overwhelming love of God that is at the heart of the transformation process that conforms us to the nature of Christ and separates us from the nature of the world.

Participation

Personal Blog, March 2014: What a wonderful week! It started off a little rough. Nisa was not feeling well, but she came around just in time for us to make the trip to the Assembly of God Fine Arts Festival for the Michigan District held in Lansing. While it was great to be able to watch so many teens on fire for God share their talents, it was even more wonderful to see Allana blossom this week. It was really about two weeks ago that she seemed to make a real breakthrough, but she certainly shined this weekend. Even after the busy two days of Fine Arts, she was up and ready to go hear Dustin Reed bring a great word at Compelled Church and then share a wonderful evening of fellowship and vision with CityLight Church. I am so thankful for God's miraculous hand in all the events of the past year and a half. I am so thankful for God's gift of perseverance during this difficult time in our lives. However, as I look at this biblical concept a little more closely, it becomes clear that God does not just provide perseverance for the tough times.

Peter, in his second recorded epistle, links the quality of perseverance to our participation in the divine nature of God. Everyone appreciates getting gifts, but how special it is when we receive a gift that extends from the very nature of the giver. So many gifts are gifts of obligation, but when the gift proceeds from the heart and represents the very being of the giver, it becomes richer and more meaningful.

> *Grace and peace be multiplied to you in the knowledge of God and of Jesus our Lord ; seeing that His divine power has granted to us everything pertaining to life and godliness, through the true knowledge of Him who called us by His own glory and excellence. For by these He has granted to us His precious and magnificent promises, so that by them you may become **partakers of the divine nature**, having escaped the corruption that is in the world by lust. Now for this very reason also,*

applying all diligence, in your faith supply moral excellence, and in your moral excellence, knowledge, and in your knowledge, self-control, and in your self-control, perseverance, and in your perseverance, godliness, and in your godliness, brotherly kindness, and in your brotherly kindness, love. For if these qualities are yours and are increasing, they render you neither useless nor unfruitful in the true knowledge of our Lord Jesus Christ (emphasis added).

—2 Pet. 1:2–8

Even more important, this gift is one that is critical to the transformation process that life in Christ Jesus brings.

And do not be conformed to this world, but be transformed by the renewing of your mind, so that you may prove what the will of God is, that which is good and acceptable and perfect.

—Rom. 12:2

But we all, with unveiled face, beholding as in a mirror the glory of the Lord, are being transformed into the same image from glory to glory, just as from the Lord, the Spirit.

—2 Cor. 3:18

It is only when we persevere, remaining under Jesus Christ, that the wonderful transformation into His spiritual image can take place. While it is a gift from God, perseverance also requires intentionality from the recipient. It is a gift that only functions when the recipient is fully focused on the giver. Pastor and author Kyle Idleman tells us in his book *Gods at War* that idols are created when gifts from God become more important than the giver. That is what happens when perseverance becomes completely focused on the events of our life (usually the negative ones) and not on Jesus Christ.

> *For You have been my help,*
> *And in the shadow of Your wings I sing for joy.*

—Ps. 63:7

Do not wait for disaster to strike to rest in the shadow of His wings. The more we remain there, the more we will experience the joy of true perseverance.

Circumstantial Evidence

circumstance
1. a fact or condition connected with or relevant to an event or action.
   "We wanted to marry, but circumstances didn't permit."
   synonyms: situation, conditions, state of affairs, position

2. one's state of financial or material welfare.
"The artists are living in reduced circumstances."
synonyms: financial position, lot, lifestyle

Allana and I recently found ourselves, through a series of conditions and facts (circumstances), short of the money that we needed to pay our bills. To be truthful, some of the conditions were not avoidable, but some of them were of our own making. I knew when I examined the situation more closely that we were going to find ourselves several hundred dollars short of the money we needed to be current. To make matters worse, Allana was not really happy about a recent major purchase I had made. I was looking at having to tell her that now (1) we were going to be late on our bills, and (2) we really must tighten up to get caught up—in fact, uncomfortably so.

There we have the circumstances in a nutshell. They are rarely simple. They are often a mix of the unavoidable, poor decisions, right decisions with consequences, and all the emotion and attitudes that human beings are prone to. While this is not about the theology of tithing, Allana and I had committed to that standard of giving. Circumstances dictated that I should hold off on my tithe until we were caught up. As I prayed over this situation, the word *hupomone* kept coming back to me. All the cute Bible studies and nice character analyses are meaningless if hupomone does not impact my life where the rubber hits the road. It is in the daily decisions and choices we make amid the circumstances that we choose the hupomone life.

Long story short, I paid our tithe first since I knew I should. Then I looked to see how bad it really was so I could tell Allana. I surveyed our accounts, and one that I rarely look at because I use it solely to pay the mortgage had several hundred extra dollars in it. Believing it was an error, I called the bank, and they confirmed that I had received a refund due to a miscalculation in the origination of our mortgage. Our bills were paid with extra to spare. The temptation is to say that even if I had not paid the tithe, the money still would have been there. Perhaps that is true, but hupomone living transcends circumstances. The real victory is spiritual, not financial. The flip side is that even if the extra money had not been provided and we had ended up late and tight, the real victory is still spiritual, not financial. Hupomone living is about making choices guided by the Holy Spirit and based in the Word of God. It is about living in our identity as children of God.

Not that I speak from want, for I have learned to be content in whatever circumstances I am. I know how to get along with humble means, and I also know how to live in prosperity; in any and every circumstance I have learned the secret of being filled and going hungry, both of having abundance and suffering need. I can do all things through Him who strengthens me. —Phil. 4:11–13

Paul did not allow his circumstances to dictate his identity. That is at the core of the hupomone life. Onesimus (see Philem. 1:16) was sent home as a runaway slave, but his identity was a brother in Christ. David was a shepherd boy, the least among his brothers, but his identity was the anointed king of Israel. Hebrews 11 walks through a litany of hupomone men and women. The people in Jesus' hometown, those who knew Him perhaps best, spoke out of His circumstances, and it blinded them to Jesus' identity as the only begotten Son of God (Luke 4:22–29). The core nature of the hupomone lifestyle transcends circumstances. It rests on the rock of Christ's identity. That is what anchors the house of the wise man, and its absence causes the foolish man's house to fall into the shifting sands. All these people walked through the fires of circumstance, the facts and conditions that stood in the face of God's will for their lives. They were not perfect (apart from Jesus), but they trusted God and not circumstance.

The Nature of God

> *Remember those who led you, who spoke*
> *the word of God to you; and considering the result*
> *of their conduct, imitate their faith. Jesus Christ is*
> *the same yesterday and today and forever. Do not*
> *be carried away by varied and strange teachings.*

—Heb. 13:7–9

Perseverance is not a trait of the human condition. While people toy with the concept—and we can point to individuals who, in limited circumstances, demonstrate a form of perseverance—they do not rise to the standard of biblical perseverance. It is for that reason that true perseverance only comes as a direct gift of God. This gift rises from Jesus' very nature. The above verses express that nature: "Jesus Christ is the same yesterday and today and forever."

Since we are forever changing, it is hard for us to conceive of an unchanging God. We do, in fact, attribute change to Him as often as we can. We seize on biblical narratives that seem to demonstrate how God has changed the way He deals with people, losing the thread of the redemptive plan set before the creation of the world. It is perhaps the only way that finite creations can conceive of an infinite Creator without childlike faith. We unwittingly demonstrate Jesus' assertion.

> And He called a child to Himself and set him before them, and said, "Truly I say to you, unless you are converted and become like children, you will not enter the kingdom of heaven. Whoever then humbles himself as this child, he is the greatest in the kingdom of heaven.

—Matt. 18:2–4

God proclaimed His divine perseverance when He declared to Moses:

> "Thus you shall say to the sons of Israel, 'I AM has sent me to you.'" God, furthermore, said to Moses, "Thus you shall say to the sons of Israel, 'The Lord, the God of your fathers, the God of Abraham, the God of Isaac, and the God of Jacob, has sent me to

19

you.' This is My name forever, and this is My memorial-name to all generations."

—Exod. 3:14–15

The eternal I AM was announcing His perseverance to all generations. The Westminster Shorter Catechism puts it this way: "God is a Spirit, infinite, eternal, and unchangeable, in his being, wisdom, power, holiness, justice, goodness, and truth."[1]

While the catechism is not scripture, I love the simplicity of its treatment of the divine, perhaps the childlike way it approaches the question of God's nature. Yet still, for all its simplicity, the nature of God is incredibly complex in its interaction with the human condition. It is this complexity that smells of change to the inquiring (but limited) mind. The complexity of the infinite as it intertwines with the finite takes on the appearance of instability, even chaos, when observed from the finite perspective. However, there is, in fact, a singularity of purpose and intent in every nuance of the relationship. This purpose is wrapped up in another concept I struggle with.

For God so loved the world, that He gave His only begotten Son, that whoever believes in Him shall not perish, but have eternal life.

—John 3:16

---

[1] Westminster Shorter Catechism (1674), https://www.ccel.org/creeds/westminster-shorter-cat.html.

It is this eternal purpose that removes the onus of circumstance from our lives when we accept with childlike faith the hupomone aspect of God's nature. It frees us from the whirlwind of circumstances and allows us to see the straight line of God's intent within the chaos of finite existence.

> *For the law of the Spirit of life in Christ Jesus has set you free from the law of sin and death.*

—Rom. 8:2

The Holy Spirit has freed us from the law of sin and death, the law of circumstance. Hupomone living is choosing to operate in the eternal through the power of the Holy Spirit, pursuing our ongoing transformation into the image of Jesus Christ.

Chapter 2

Practical Hupomone

What then shall we say to these things? If God is for us, who is against us? He who did not spare His own Son, but delivered Him over for us all, how will He not also with Him freely give us all things? Who will bring a charge against God's elect? God is the one who justifies; who is the one who condemns? Christ Jesus is He who died, yes, rather who was raised, who is at the right hand of God, who also intercedes for us. Who will separate us from the love of Christ? Will tribulation, or distress, or persecution, or famine, or nakedness, or peril, or sword? Just as it is written,

"FOR YOUR SAKE WE ARE BEING PUT TO DEATH ALL DAY LONG; WE WERE CONSIDERED AS SHEEP TO BE SLAUGHTERED."

But in all these things we overwhelmingly conquer through Him who loved us. For I am convinced that neither death, nor life, nor angels, nor principalities, nor things present, nor things to come, nor powers, nor height, nor depth, nor any other created thing, will

be able to separate us from the love of God,
which is in Christ Jesus our Lord.

—Romans 8:31–39

A friend of mine paid me a great compliment and asked me a personal question. "How do you stay the same as the world happens around you? So many people I know turn cynical. You are always kind and ready to help." I must admit that unfortunately I gave this person the wrong answer. It focused on the situation at hand and not on my identity in Jesus Christ. Why did I give the wrong answer? Why did I not intuitively know what the correct answer was?

I pondered this for several days before writing this chapter. I absolutely believe this question came to me through my friend by the hand of God. My friend did not realize that the question and the observance behind it answered a question I have been asking God for some time—What is the value of this idea, these disciplines that You have placed so strongly in me? What is, practically speaking, hupomone living?

So here is my answer to that question:

> *For this reason also, since the day we heard* of it, *we*
> *have not ceased to pray for you and to ask that you*
> *may be filled with the knowledge of His will in all*
> *spiritual wisdom and understanding, so that you will*
> *walk in a manner worthy of the Lord, to please* Him
> *in all respects, bearing fruit in every good work and*

increasing in the knowledge of God; strengthened with all power, according to His glorious might, for the attaining of all steadfastness and patience; joyously giving thanks to the Father, who has qualified us to share in the inheritance of the saints in Light. —Col. 1:9–12

Paul, powered by the inspiration of the Holy Spirit, is brilliant here. This passage contains a prayer, direction, promise, and thanksgiving. We find in this passage the core of hupomone.

The prayer for ourselves and our brothers and sisters in Christ is that we all would be filled with the knowledge of God's will, not as the world (or even the church) sees it, but through the lens of spiritual wisdom and understanding as only comes from regular interaction with the Holy Spirit. It is this spiritual understanding that frees us from circumstance and opens up the very possibility of the hupomone lifestyle.

The direction is that we walk in a manner worthy of the Lord. When I was a young man, my constant question to God was, "What can I get away with, and how far can I go without having Your hammer drop on me?" That led me far from hupomone living. Then I began to see Him and ask, "What can I do that will be 'in a manner worthy' of You, Lord?" "What can I do today to please You?" Paul fleshed this out later in Colossians, but just coming to the place of asking the question—praying the question—was a big step in the right direction. It began to eliminate my reaction to circumstance in favor of my submission to God.

The promise is twofold. The implicit promise is that when we truly pursue the hupomone life, we will please Him, bear fruit, increase in our knowledge of Him, and be strengthened, not according to our understanding or our circumstances but in accordance with His. As we pursue Him, He pursues us. It is an incredible upward spiral of relationship with God. It leads to joyously giving thanks to God, not because of circumstances but as a result of relationship and identity. It is on this that the explicit promise rests—we *are* qualified to share in the inheritance of the saints of Light. The rest of the passage references our future, but all of that is based on His past—"the Father, who has qualified us" (Col. 1:12). Paul goes on to say, "For He rescued us from the domain of darkness, and transferred us to the kingdom of His beloved Son, in whom we have redemption, the forgiveness of sins" (Col. 1:13–14). It is on this that hupomone living rests. We are not here to react to circumstances; we are here to walk worthy, please Him, bear fruit, be strengthened, and live as those qualified by God to be heirs along with our Lord and Savior Jesus Christ.

Results

Now I want you to know, brethren, that my circumstances have turned out for the greater progress of the gospel.

—Phil. 1:12

hupomone
steadfastness, constancy, endurance
In the New Testament, the characteristic of a man
who is not swerved from his deliberate purpose and
his loyalty to faith and piety by even the greatest
trials and sufferings
patiently and steadfastly
a patient, steadfast waiting for
a patient enduring, sustaining perseverance

Hupomone living frees us from the circumstances of life.
We are no longer bound to react to circumstance after
circumstance. Instead, as Brother Lawrence wrote in his
book *The Practice of the Presence of God*, we are free to
practice the presence of God. We are able to make our
relationship with Him our total focus. We also cannot make
our circumstances the foundation of our faith; that will
distract from the singular purpose of pursuing God and
result in a faith that is blown here and there by the
situational waves of life (see Eph. 4:14).

> *Are they servants of Christ?—I speak as if insane—I
> more so; in far more labors, in far more
> imprisonments, beaten times without number, often
> in danger of death. Five times I received from the
> Jews thirty-nine lashes. Three times I was beaten
> with rods, once I was stoned, three times I was
> shipwrecked, a night and a day I have spent in the
> deep.* I have been *on frequent journeys, in dangers
> from rivers, dangers from robbers, dangers from my
> countrymen, dangers from the Gentiles, dangers in*

the city, dangers in the wilderness, dangers on the
sea, dangers among false brethren.

—2 Cor. 11:23–26

Paul goes on to list the circumstances of his life as a missionary and even the intense times of communion with God as well as his "thorn in the flesh" (2 Cor. 12:7). Paul could boast in his hupomone lifestyle, that he endured all these things and was graced by intense visions from God. In the end analysis, Paul understood, perhaps along with the author of Ecclesiastes, that this, too, is vanity. It is better to boast in weakness and recognize that the important thing is that the power of Christ dwells inside us. Paul understood that when he rejected circumstances as the guide and measure of his life and practiced the presence of Jesus Christ in every situation, whatever happened to him "turned out for the greater progress of the gospel" (Phil. 1:12). That is the result of the hupomone lifestyle. It is the goal that transcends our individual personalities, situations, callings, theologies, denominations, socioeconomic statuses, and so on.

When we enter the hupomone life, we are freed not only from circumstances but also from results. It is a natural result of who we are as children of God and the natural excellence that occurs when we focus on pursuing God. It is the natural conclusion of Romans 8:28: "And we know that God causes all things to work together for good to those who love God, to those who are called according to His purpose." However, we are not freed from the need to pursue all we do with excellence. Over and over, scripture calls for Christ followers to reach for excellence. Unfortunately, I have actually heard intentional incompetence lauded as a way to encourage the work of the Holy Spirit in one's life. This is directly contradicted in scripture.

> *Be diligent to present yourself approved to God as a workman who does not need to be ashamed, accurately handling the word of truth.*

—2 Tim. 2:15

> *Now for this very reason also, applying all diligence, in your faith supply moral excellence, and in your moral excellence, knowledge,*

—2 Pet. 1:5

> *Whether, then, you eat or drink or whatever you do, do all to the glory of God.*

—1 Cor. 10:31

The fact that we are freed from the constraints of results allows us to focus our pursuit of excellence where it belongs, on our relationship with Jesus Christ and our desire to bring our heavenly Father glory.

Walking in the Miraculous

I wrote this section of the chapter several years ago. But it became much more meaningful over the years as Allana and I walked through the storm of leukemia and a bone marrow transplant. Though I did not write this as part of my examination of perseverance, it fits tightly with this study because at its core, persevering as a Christian *is* walking in the miraculous. When we truly remain under Christ Jesus as the covering for our lives, the miraculous is bound to show its face. "Open the eyes of my heart Lord," goes the popular song refrain. Open my eyes to see Your miraculous hand in and around my life every day.

> *So then, does He who provides you with the Spirit and works miracles among you, do it by the works of the Law, or by hearing with faith?*

> —Gal. 3:5

A big part of me wants to live on the basis of logical observation instead of spiritual expectation. But God is teaching me to walk in the miraculous. When we truly hear the gospel with faith, there should be an expectation of the miraculous. It is part of the package. It is not a mystical toy store or the ability to bend God's power to our will for our happiness. It is simply expecting God to act, walking out our faith, and then watching Him move and work in and around us.

The cool thing is that the miraculous looks a little different every time. When something miraculous happens in our lives, we often make the mistake of running around expecting the very same thing to happen over and over or even just one more time. That may be because we want to control the miraculous. Humanity has always had an inherent fear of the things we cannot control. We think it's better to have a god who responds to our requests exactly the same way all of the time and speaks into our lives in the ways we want him to instead of sanctifying us and ever conforming us more and more to the mind of Christ.

The author of Hebrews reveals the purpose of the miraculous.

> *How will we escape if we neglect so great a salvation? After it was at the first spoken through the Lord, it was confirmed to us by those who heard, God also testifying with them, both by signs and wonders and by various miracles and by gifts of the Holy Spirit according to His own will.*
>
> —Heb. 2:3–4

It confirms to us our salvation. It is similar to Paul's statement in Galatians 3:5, which we already looked at.

The other amazing thing is that God will not be put in a box. Sometimes we mistake the fact that He is the same yesterday, today, and tomorrow for the fact that we will be able to manipulate and predict His actions in our lives. This error is revealed in Isaiah:

> "For My thoughts are not your thoughts,
> Nor are your ways My ways," declares the LORD.
> "For as the heavens are higher than the earth,
> So are My ways higher than your ways
> And my thoughts than your thoughts."

—Isa. 55:8–9

Does that mean we just drift along being pushed here and there by a capricious God? Not at all! We cry out our needs, concerns, suffering, and desires to God and then open our spiritual eyes wide and watch Him work. It will be amazing, often in ways we least expect.

Change

> Jesus Christ is the same yesterday and today and forever.

—Heb. 13:8

The fancy word for this section is *immutability*. But that is the last time you will see it here. The Bible tells us that in a world of change, biblical perseverance calls for a unique constancy from Christ-followers. God declares His own character when he tells Moses, "I AM WHO I AM" (Exod. 3:14). This Hebrew phrase, which became the very name of

31

God to Israel, declares His eternal constancy. It is here that we find one of the prime qualities of biblical perseverance for the believer.

> *For those whom He foreknew, He also predestined* to become *conformed to the image of His Son, so that He would be the firstborn among many brethren.*

—Rom. 8:29

It is only by this miraculous transformation process and the submission of our will to His will that we begin our journey to biblical perseverance. So do we live in the same place, do the same things, and never change what we eat or do for the rest of our live? Clearly not. We do not even have that kind of control over the circumstances of our lives. Change is introduced to our existence every day, every hour, and every minute of our lives here on earth. This is where we see that biblical perseverance is a spiritual gift, not a physical effort. It cannot be faked or practiced by human effort. It is manifested in the lives of those who serve and have a personal relationship with God.

Consider Daniel.

> *Then the king ordered Ashpenaz, the chief of his officials, to bring in some of the sons of Israel, including some of the royal family and of the nobles. Now among them from the sons of Judah were Daniel, Hananiah, Mishael and Azariah. Then the*

commander of the officials assigned new *names to them; and to Daniel he assigned* the name *Belteshazzar, to Hananiah Shadrach, to Mishael Meshach and to Azariah Abed-nego.*

—Dan. 1:3, 6

Talk about change! As a young man, Daniel was ripped from his home, dragged halfway across the known world, and even had his name taken away. This Babylonian tactic was specifically designed to destroy perseverance. Do not be deceived; the Enemy is out to destroy your perseverance. He wants you to come out from under the covering of Christ where he can have a clear and open shot at you. The Babylonians did everything they could to shake Daniel's identity as a child of God. But what happened?

> *But Daniel made up his mind that he would not defile himself with the king's choice food or with the wine which he drank; so he sought* permission *from the commander of the officials that he might not defile himself.* —Dan. 1:8

Amid all this change, Daniel did not change. It is important to note that Daniel remained under Jesus Christ in every aspect of his behavior. That brings us to another important aspect of biblical perseverance. It always expresses the character of God.

> *But the fruit of the Spirit is love, joy, peace, patience, kindness, goodness, faithfulness, gentleness, self-*

control; against such things there is no law. Now those who belong to Christ Jesus have crucified the flesh with its passions and desires. If we live by the Spirit, let us also walk by the Spirit. Let us not become boastful, challenging one another, envying one another.

—Gal. 5:22–26

Biblical perseverance is never rude or arrogant. Perseverance that does not fall in line with God's Word is not biblical and is not godly. When we truly walk in biblical perseverance, we are like a lighthouse in the storm. We go on to read about Daniel:

Now God granted Daniel favor and compassion in the sight of the commander of the officials. As for these four youths, God gave them knowledge and intelligence in every branch of literature and wisdom; Daniel even understood all kinds of visions and dreams.

—Dan. 1:9, 17

But let there be no mistake. Satan *hates* biblical perseverance and believes he can destroy it. Daniel continued to face opposition throughout his life. Many other saints, both biblical and historical, persevered to martyrdom. Regardless of the physical outcome, the spiritual truth remains the same, and the lighthouse of faithfulness shines in the darkness.

Chapter 3

19 Days – The Beginning of Hupomone

*Even though I walk through the valley of the
shadow of death,
I fear no evil, for You are with me;
Your rod and Your staff, they comfort me.*

—Psalm 23:4

Nineteen days. Who knew that 19 days would ever come to be so meaningful to me? The short background for the 19 days is couched in expectation, pain, and blood. From 2003—when our daughter Chayla was born—through 2012, Allana had seven miscarriages. Those years and those losses brought Allana and me both emotional and physical suffering. They generated fear and a deep sense of emptiness. After multiple failed promises of resolution by multiple medical professionals, we were simply labeled "unable to carry to term." We cycled through periods of failed faith, guilt that we did not have enough faith, and attempts to claim and speak into being each child who found his or her way to heaven instead of into our arms. The 19 days represent the realization of on incredible miracle in our lives and the beginning of another.

Day 1 will forever be a joyous day. Year after year, we celebrate that day—the birth of Nisa Faith. Day 1 was the culmination of nine years of loss and nine months of a mélange of concern, faith, fear, trust, and surrender. It was a day of arrival, of life, of completion. It was a day of overt blessing. December 16, 2012, was a joyous day. What Allana and I did not know, what we could not have known, was that it was a day of provision, a day of strength given. I would be lying if I said that I sat at this computer with a solid thesis or a planned allegory. The reality is that this is my first opportunity to truly experience and embrace the 19 days. When they occurred, they were simply another 19 days in the Christmas season, and in 2013, we were still too deeply embroiled in Allana's battle against leukemia and her recovery from the bone marrow transplant for me to experience them the way I am this year.

Day 1 was not without its difficulties. Ask any mother, and she will tell you that this joy comes with its own brand of pain. Recently, two dear friends who are expecting engaged in a tongue-in-cheek argument on Facebook concerning any man's ability to truly conceive of the trials and eventual pain of pregnancy and birth. I do not even pretend (or desire) to really understand, preferring to stand by Allana's side than in her place for this event. Chayla's birth nine years ago had been a stroll in the park. Nisa's birth was more like a kick in the gut and then a short sprint to the finish line—a race in which Nisa beat our doctor and surprised our nurse. Still, there she was: perfect, beautiful, a miracle from the hand of God. We basked in the joy of the now. We knew it was Day 1, but we didn't know there were only 18 days left in this paragraph of our lives.

The frenzy of the night (Nisa was born at 9:40 p.m.) and the flush of the first day gave way to a wash of relief. The tensions of the past nine months, the fear at each ultrasound appointment, the anticipation of a pronouncement that a new cycle of loss and grief had begun—they all fell away. There was tremendous thanksgiving and praise throughout the many who prayed for us, who supported us through this pregnancy and, in many cases, our multiple losses.

We joyfully prepared to bring Nisa home. I am not sure my words can express Day 2 any better than the twinkle in Allana's eyes. This Christmas gift was probably the best we had ever received. The whole family rejoiced at the absence of those fateful "talks" when we had lost so many other children. Each of us in our own way processed the losses of the past in the joyous light of Nisa's arrival. We couldn't help thinking of Nisa's siblings in heaven, from the crashing resonation of Josiah's passing (our first loss and first introduction to the idea that not every pregnancy ends with a babe in your arms) to the unheralded passing of Ezra Matthew (our final loss, an early miscarriage). Day 2 became about rest, enjoyment, and blessing. The gathering storm was still beyond the horizon. There was no sense of the deadly changes perhaps just beginning to take place. Still, what would come did not erase the joy and peace of Day 2. It only served to highlight it and to make me more thankful than ever for God's grace.

The frenzied posting, calling, and e-mailing were over. Nisa Faith had been announced to the world. As we approached the day that we celebrate our Savior's birth, we finally got to truly celebrate Nisa's coming. Facebook began to respond.

> *D. A. Precious: And those cheeks! I'm so happy for you!*
> *December 19, 2012, at 1:48 am · Like*
>
> *Allana Belrose Guidry: I know. They are getting lots of kisses*
> *December 19, 2012, at 1:54 am · Like · 2*

Nisa's cheeks were getting a lot of kisses. Allana was feeling a little more tired than usual, but then she just had a baby, and she was not as young as she used to be.

We were prepared for all the life changes that a newborn brings—bassinet, Pack 'n Play, bottles, formula, car seat, diapers, and more, all in place. What we did not know was that God had also prepared us for the changes that most likely, even on this day two years ago, were beginning to take place in the depths of Allana's bones (weird to type that and not mean it metaphorically). Eleven years of growth through struggle as a family, as individuals, and as children of the living God were about to be tested in a way we had not imagined, even in our wildest nightmares. Even as we prepared for Nisa's arrival, God was preparing us for something we could not have even begun to be ready for. There were so many crossroads where God directed what seemed a long and windy path. It seemed so foolish, as foolish as buying diapers and preparing a nursery for a baby who would never come.

Nisa was here, and the long and windy path would soon be clear.

> *For we do not have a high priest who cannot sympathize with our weaknesses, but One who has been tempted in all things as we are, yet without sin. Therefore let us draw near with confidence to the throne of grace, so that we may receive mercy and find grace to help in time of need.*

—Heb. 4:15–16

My original intent was to follow these 19 days day by day. That did not happen, for a variety of reasons. One is certainly that processing the events of two years ago, now removed from the rigorous exigencies of Allana's treatments and bone marrow transplant recovery, is not as structured, neat, and clean as I thought it might be. As we passed through this season, I watched each of us quietly working through our feelings. When the busyness of the holidays passed for a minute and routine life emerged, the stress of this process appeared in a variety of fashions. Still, as a family, we had the deep assurance that God was in control and that we have an eternal High Priest in His presence interceding on our behalf.

The frenzy of birth faded in the light of our celebration of our Savior's arrival on the scene. Those days were filled with wonderful preparation and quiet enjoyment (with little sleep). We were blessed by the generosity of so many—many who will read this book—as we were suddenly and unexpectedly blessed that year. Then, as now, I did not know why I was surprised when I prayed for provision and it came in abundance. Presents were wrapped as Nisa was loved and coddled by so many. The preparations made over the previous month were in full use. Allana was enjoying her Christmas blessing, drinking in Nisa's presence having desired this particular beverage for so very long.

Allana woke on Day 7, a little sore, her throat a bit raspy, and maybe just a touch of fever. Not to worry, she did just give birth, and the crazy weather was enough to make anyone a bit down.

The preparations made over a lifetime by an all-knowing God were about to be tested. Quiet joy and praises rose from home and ministry wrapped in one. So much had been put on hold as we waited for Nisa. We were already making plans for spring and summer, mapping out what our lives and ministry would look like. We did not know that in less than two weeks, everything would change. But God had been molding us into "change managers" for some time. Early on our journey to full-time ministry, after I left the hospitality industry, God gave me a word—He said I would only know what I would be doing and how we would be living 30 days at a time. It was frustrating and difficult, but it prepared me for the runaway train ride that was coming.

Allana's fever worsened. We moved through Christmas and toward the New Year. Her sore throat spread to body aches and stomach pain. Those days, the days everything changed, are barely a blur in my memory. I can remember little of what happened outside of the progression of the illness we did not even know was there. Even with the fever and discomfort, there was a blissful ignorance of the journey we were being called to embark on. To put the whole piece into perspective, Nisa was born at 9:40 p.m. on December 16, 2012. The 17th was Day 1, and we moved on from there. Now we are looking at December 25th through January 1st. As I review the various posts on Facebook, I see faces of joy and innocence. The fever is a footnote to the joy of the season that was made even more joyful by the arrival of our miracle baby. Allana even downplayed the intensity of the fevers, putting them at 102. By the night of December 31st, they were spiking between 104 and 106, or maybe not wanting to worry her too much, I fudged the numbers a little (I do not really remember). A trip to the emergency room was forestalled only by the fact that the ibuprofen was knocking them down to safer territory.

By New Year's Day, it was enough. We called Allana's obstetrician's office. The doctor on call prescribed a heavy-duty antibiotic and some anti-nausea medicine to mitigate the side-effects. We started the medications right away, but, of course, Allana did not get better. By January 2nd, she was extremely sick. The pain in her belly had gotten much worse. We suspected a postpartum infection but did not understand why the antibiotics were not helping. January 3rd was a Thursday. We arrived at the doctor's office at 10:00 a.m. and were ushered into the examining room. Our nurse practitioner listened patiently to the story, but as the physical exam progressed, her demeanor changed. There was an urgency to her motions as she felt the abnormal swelling in Allana's belly, the tenderness, and the lumps at her joints. I could feel my apprehension rising, but there were so many pills, shots, and treatments that I was sure a quick fix was in order.

"I have called the Flower Hospital," she announced. "They are expecting her."

"What? We need to get some tests?"

"No, we are admitting her."

"We have plans. Can it wait until Monday?"

"No, I want you there within two hours. Go home, settle the children, and pick up what you need. Once you are there, they will begin running tests to see what is going on."

It was not until late in the evening that I heard the word *leukemia* for the first time, mixed in with a couple other potential causes for Allana's test results. When a hematologist said, "I am hoping this is a severe case of mononucleosis," the tension began to rise in earnest. I began making phone calls, preparing our prayer warriors for a battle I prayed was not coming.

If the fevers were the relentless clacking as the roller coaster climbs the first rise, then this was the ominous pause before the first drop. Friday morning, the hematologist entered the room. There were tears in his eyes as he approached Allana and me where we were sitting on the hospital bed with Nisa. Nothing could have softened his statement: "I am sorry, but Allana has leukemia. We will be starting chemotherapy as soon as it can be prepared." We looked down at our little Nisa. The questions raged in our minds. I had seen the ravages of chemotherapy since I worked in a hospital for a few years. Allana had not, but she understood that a long hospital stay was coming. Then our thoughts went to our children at home. This is similar but so different from sharing our losses. What to say? When to say it? We were falling down that first drop of the roller coaster now, and everything was spinning around us, leaving us little time to think. However, as our emotions and physical beings rode the speeding rails, God remained rock solid and faithful. The outpouring of love from God's people was incredible. Even amid the myriad of "spiritual" advisers who decried our lack of faith for starting treatment or saw this as a sign of trouble in our walk with God, we were overwhelmed by God's love. "Traveling deeper and deeper, closer and closer to God"— Allana's words rang with truth in a way that neither of us could ever imagine. Deeper and deeper. Closer, closer to God...there was nowhere else to go.

> The LORD is my shepherd,
> I shall not want.
> He makes me lie down in green pastures;
> He leads me beside quiet waters.
> He restores my soul;
> He guides me in the paths of righteousness
> For His name's sake.

Even though I walk through the valley of the shadow of death,
I fear no evil, for You are with me;
Your rod and Your staff, they comfort me.
You prepare a table before me in the presence of my enemies;
You have anointed my head with oil;
My cup overflows.
Surely goodness and lovingkindness will follow me all the days of my life,
And I will dwell in the house of the LORD forever.

—Ps. 23

The Lord is my Shepherd, I shall not want.

This premise is a must. It is not a theory, a cute saying, or even a prayerful wish. It is only when you function within this spiritual truth without regard to apparent circumstances that you can look back at the 19 days without fear. This passage, of course, would be out of step if it were talking about a fulfillment of all my personal desires. The translation of the Hebrew word *chacer* here as "want" is unfortunate in a modern translation. The word is really about lacking basic needs (not even cultural and certainly not the "me" generational concept of needs). It could even be translated "become empty." Sodom and Gomorrah were destroyed because they lacked (*chacer*) 10 righteous men. The reality is that the Shepherd does not serve the wants (desires) of His flock. He serves the needs of His flock as He guides them in His wisdom and for His purposes. It is when we release our own will to the

44

Shepherd that we rest in the assurance that we will never "become empty."

So here is the reality of the 19 days. We never know when we are living them out. My family is not unique in this experience. I would guess that every one of you has walked through your own 19 days, innocent of the storm that was just over the horizon. The fact is that this was not my first journey through the 19 days, but it was my first journey through them where I truly understood David's heart as he penned this psalm. How we walk out the 19 days is a function of this psalm. Sentence by sentence, it is a guide written by a man who walked through his own 19 days many times over.

He makes me lie down in green pastures.

What a lovely picture in words. We can all envision ourselves lying in luxurious grass, running our hands through it and wiggling our toes. I certainly do not want to ruin your reverie, but let's get back to the imagery of David's psalm. It is easy to do when we go back to the Hebrew language. *Deshe' Naveh* is translated "green pastures." The imagery is a little more direct and specific. *Deshe'* is not the color green but specifically refers to fresh grass as opposed to withered, dry grass. It is the kind of grass that a shepherd would recognize as healthy and nutritious for his sheep. *Naveh* is a specific reference to a dwelling place for both sheep and shepherd. Nathan the prophet told David that it was God who took him from the sheep and the *Naveh* that made him king. Scripture repeatedly uses this word for the Lord's "habitation" or "dwelling place." *Deshe' Naveh* is not about a fuzzy, feel-good place; it is about a place that promotes real health and wellness for us in the presence of our great Shepherd, in the presence of our God. Like sheep, we are all too ready to eat whatever toxic plants look good at the moment (yes, sheep will poison themselves if left in an environment where plants are toxic to them). It is only when we follow our Shepherd that we will find the *Deshe' Naveh* we so desperately need.

By now you are probably asking what this has to do with the 19 days. It is easy to see and feel the *Deshe' Naveh* in the sunny calm of the 19 days. Too often we spend the 19 days wiggling our toes in the grass instead of taking in the nutrition and wellness that is the provision of the Good Shepherd. Then, when the fuzzy comfort of the sunshine is suddenly replaced by the bitterness of the storm, we think the *Deshe' Naveh* is gone, and we run. Like silly sheep, we run from the very place of health and wellness that God has made our habitation—we run because of some wind, thunder, lightning, and rain. We are tempted to eat the toxic greenery just because there it feels like the sun is shining. We break our legs in the rocky crags as we run to what appears to be shelter. Will the Good Shepherd track us down and beckon us back to the *Deshe' Naveh*, even carry us while we heal? Amen and Amen! Yes! But God also honors our free will, and if we do not surrender to the arms of the Shepherd, the results can be devastating to all.

I pray true health and wellness for you all. May you always choose to rest with your Shepherd in the *Deshe' Naveh*.

He leads me beside quiet waters.

I have only been whitewater rafting once, and it was in the middle of a terrible summer drought, so what should have been a harrowing, exciting, and somewhat dangerous adventure turned out to be more of a stroll in the park on a sunny day. I know that this same river in other seasons has been dangerous to the point of claiming lives. The rivers and streams of David's Israel were just as changeable. One minute they could be quiet streams bubbling along, and then a cloud burst, perhaps not even in the immediate vicinity, could swell them to deadly proportions. The "quiet waters" is probably a reference to the many small springs throughout the land of Israel. Cool, clean, and refreshing, these springs were a safe place of comfort for thirsty sheep.

God desires to lead us in places of refreshing safety on paths of restoration and righteousness that fulfill His purpose for His people. Enjoying the rest and nutrition of the green pastures and following our Great Shepherd beside the quiet, refreshing, restoring waters of His grace and love are spiritual disciplines. There is a temptation during the 19 days to believe that we do not need to walk in the Spirit. Everything seems wonderful. Nothing could happen to steal the joy and peace we feel. When we place ourselves in that frame of mind, we begin to rely on the circumstances of our life instead of our Great Shepherd for our well-being. David makes it clear that the pastures and waters are not about circumstances.

He restores my soul; He guides me in the paths of righteousness for His name's sake.

Righteousness and restoration are about our relationship with God. Here is the hook. Since the pasture and the waters are not about circumstances, we are no less resting in green pastures on Day 20 than we were on Day 2. Just because we have a situational change (even a drastic one), the reality of the spiritual disciplines of the pasture and the waters is not impacted whatsoever. However, it does not *feel* that way. If we could just ride the whole way on our feeling of well-being, then it would not involve spiritual discipline. When I was holding Nisa and rejoicing in well-being as Christmas approached, and as we felt gifted beyond belief, the pasture and the waters seemed a no-brainer. When I sat on that hospital bed with my wife's health failing beside me and heard the words "I am sorry, Allana has leukemia," and then "I am sorry but the leukemia is Philadelphia positive, without a bone marrow transplant," everything seemed to change. The pasture vanished; the waters became bitter—or had they?

Even though I walk through the valley of the shadow of death, I fear no evil, for You are with me; Your rod and Your staff, they comfort me.

The valley of the shadow of death is about circumstance. The verbs in Hebrew are all in the same tense, except for "anointed." They all indicate current and ongoing action. The green pastures and still waters do not vanish because

48

we are in the valley. If we focus on His rod of guidance and His staff of protection, the nourishing green grass of His Word and the refreshing waters of His Spirit remain as we walk the path of righteousness, because none of it depends on me or on my circumstances. It all depends on *His name*.

> *And there is salvation in no one else; for there is no other name under heaven that has been given among men by which we must be saved.*

> —Acts 4:12

Enjoy the green pastures and still waters *today*!

He restores my soul; He guides me in the paths of righteousness for His Name's sake.

The nature of biblical Hebrew poetry is repetitive. This form can serve three functions. It creates a literary elegance that is aesthetically pleasing. It emphasizes the thought the poet is trying to convey. It also allows the poet to clarify the thought being conveyed, particularly when the first iteration is a metaphor. In the first two verses of Psalm 23, David offers one of the most universally recognized biblical metaphors—"the LORD is my shepherd." In verse 3, David opens his heart and repeats the metaphor in the plain words of his experience—"He restores my soul; He guides me in the paths of righteousness for His name's sake." There is a temptation to equate the green pastures and the quiet waters with the circumstances of our lives. This can be a trap of the 19 days. We can begin to believe that the

49

restoration of our souls and the righteousness of our lives are tied up in how things are going. That is especially easy when things are going great. We read, "He makes me lie down in green pastures" and say, "Wow! The green pastures are the thing. As long as I am in green pastures, I am going to be okay. In fact, I am going to do everything I can to stay in green pastures." The hook is that when we do this, we stop following God. The green pastures are not about our life circumstances; they are about God.

"He restores my soul." The path along the quiet waters, the path of righteousness is not about us and where we are; it is about who is our guide. In fact, David goes on to talk about circumstances.

"Even though I walk through the valley of the shadow of death, I fear no evil, for You are with me; Your rod and Your staff, they comfort me." When I first read through this with the 19 days in mind, I thought, "Here it is, Day 20—been there done that." But as I began to pray about it, God gently told me that Day 20 is no different. Why is the rod and the staff so comforting? They symbolize authority, power, and support. Is it that God will thunder into the valley and beat back all the darkness? Perhaps David's Jewish superhero was the Shepherd from the comics he read as a boy. Maybe he had lightning bolts firing from his rod and his staff crashing down with the power of an earthquake. But that does not fit the metaphor. What did the Good Shepherd use his rod and his staff to do? We only need to step back to the beginning of David's beautiful poetry. "He makes me lie down in green pastures; He leads me beside quiet waters. He restores my soul; He guides me in the paths of righteousness for His name's sake." Sorry, no thunderous rescue.

The reality is that our circumstances do not change the behavior of our God. Even though I walk through the valley of the shadow of death, I fear no evil, for He is with me; His rod and His staff comfort me. They make me lie down in green pastures. They lead me beside still waters. Take comfort. Whether in the 19 days, the years that precede them, or the days that follow them, God is God, and He is our Great Shepherd. If you follow the direction of His rod and His staff, you will find yourself in green pastures, beside still waters. Your soul will be restored, no matter how battered it is, and you will find yourself on the path of righteousness, not by any effort of your own but by the direction of the only One who can lead you home.

You prepare a table before me in the presence of my enemies.

David knew about enemies. He faced them in a literal way that few of us have ever experienced (and most of us will never experience). Whether it was the giant Goliath or his own son Absalom, David's life was filled with the turmoil that mortal enemies bring. We are unlikely to face an armored giant or have our son plot to steal everything we have, but the enemies we face are just as real as those that assaulted David's peace. Sometimes we are our own worst enemy. Other times, the simple fact that we are God's people in an ungodly world places us in the presence of our enemies. God's table provided sustenance and hospitality in the presence of those who hated David, and it provides the same for us. It *is* God's table. He does not call us to prepare our own tables in enemy territory. He calls us to sit at *His* table under the covering of *His* hospitality. Just as wisdom prepares a place for those who seek God (see Prov. 9), God has prepared this haven in the midst of our turmoil.

David says "in the presence of." That is a concept that too many Christians just do not get and too many preachers and teachers ignore. It is attractive to us to just avoid the whole "valley of the shadow of death" idea. Certainly, we say, if I pray right and have enough faith, I can just stay on the mountaintop all the time. When Allana was first diagnosed with cancer, we had several very well-meaning brothers and sisters in Christ who assumed that if we just prayed and had faith, she would be instantly and miraculously healed. Now do not get me wrong; I completely believe that God does heal. I also believe that God intervened on many occasions throughout our journey through cancer. However, when Allana and I prayed and sought God, especially after her first round of chemotherapy, His answer was, "I need you to walk through the valley of the shadow of death. My rod and My staff will comfort you. I will prepare a table in the presence of your enemies. You will dwell in My house forever."

The fruit that has come from walking in the valley has been utterly amazing. God has provided opportunity after opportunity for us to share Him with so many people. Here is the cool thing about the tradition of hospitality in Old Testament times—strangers were welcome at the table. The table that God has prepared for us "in the presence of my enemies" is one that we are free to invite *all* to join. It is not a table that we are supposed to wall off or cower under. It is a place to introduce our enemies to our most gracious (literally full of grace) host, Jesus Christ our Savior and Lord. Who will you invite to sit at God's table?

Chapter 4

Daniel and the Long Haul

As for every matter of wisdom and understanding about which the king consulted them, he found them ten times better than all the magicians and *conjurers who were in all his realm. And Daniel continued until the first year of Cyrus the king.*

—Daniel 1:20–21

Daniel is one of the most amazing characters in the Bible for several reasons. Our canon of scripture places Daniel among the prophets, but the Jewish scriptures do not. The Jewish canon places the book of Daniel in a group called The Writings. While one cannot deny Daniel's prophetic gift, he did not hold the office of prophet. Certainly, God calls on him repeatedly to speak to the various leaders of Babylon, but that leads us to another unique thing about Daniel. Other than the fact that Daniel was a Jew and was taken at a young age from his home in Judah, the contents of the book of Daniel do not speak of or to the Jews.

So what do we know about this enigmatic figure and author of one of the 39 books of the Old Testament (one of the 24 in the Jewish canon)? Daniel lived in the sixth century BC. His family was either of the royal family or the nobility.

Almost everything we know about Daniel comes from the book bearing his name. The authorship of the book is much debated, but I do not doubt that Daniel wrote it near the end of his life, probably after he retired from public service. I find most other textual criticism to be contrived either for academic reasons (you have to write your dissertation on something) or with the express need to explain away the miraculous.

Daniel grew up during hard times in Judah. His dedication to God from the very beginning indicates that his parents were godly people living in ungodly times. They are not mentioned here or elsewhere in scripture. If they did survive the siege and capture of Jerusalem, Daniel was taken from them at around the age of 13. That was the typical age when the Babylonians of that era began training to become public servants. We are able to historically place the siege and capture of Jerusalem around the year 605 BC. That enables us to date many aspects of Daniel's life, particularly when his service to Babylon began and ended. That is what caught my attention and brought me to look a little deeper at the life of this man of God, this Hupomone Man.

Daniel, as I said, was not a prophet, and he was not a priest or a missionary. He was a public administrator and, in many ways, a politician by trade. Daniel served God in the Babylonian courts and government until the year or year after Cyrus captured Babylon and seized control of that empire. That event is historically established as occurring in 540 BC. So Daniel served God in his capacity as an administrator for several versions of the Neo-Babylonian Empire, from 605 BC until 540 BC, or, including training, around 65 years. That is some serious hupomone! Throughout that time, Daniel maintained his dedication to and love for God, even in the face of death. He probably spent the last few years of his life (from about 540 to 543 BC) penning the book under the inspiration of the Holy Spirit. It would become part of the canon of scripture we have as the Word of God today. He was very much an Old Testament missionary, called to a pagan people to speak the heart of God. Consider his words to Nebuchadnezzar:

> Therefore, O king, may my advice be pleasing to you: break away now from your sins by doing righteousness and from your iniquities by showing mercy to the poor, in case there may be a prolonging of your prosperity.

—Dan. 4:27

It seems that studies of Daniel usually focus on either the eschatological aspects of his prophecies or just a few specific events in the book.

Hope

What are the characteristics of someone who stays in it for the long haul with God? Specifically, what can we see in Daniel's life that contributed to the fact that he outlasted kings and empires? The first thing we are going to look at is *hope*. Even though the word is never used in the text of the book of Daniel, Daniel's hope in God still shines through. Consider this prayer of thanks after God revealed Nebuchadnezzar's dream:

> Daniel said,
>
>> "Let the name of God be blessed forever and ever,
>> For wisdom and power belong to Him.
>> It is He who changes the times and the epochs;
>> He removes kings and establishes kings;
>> He gives wisdom to wise men
>> And knowledge to men of understanding.
>> It is He who reveals the profound and hidden things;
>> He knows what is in the darkness,
>> And the light dwells with Him.
>> To You, O God of my fathers, I give thanks and praise,
>> For You have given me wisdom and power;
>> Even now You have made known to me what we requested of You,
>> For You have made known to us the king's matter."

—Dan. 2:20–23

Daniel makes it clear to Nebuchadnezzar who the revealer of mysteries is—God, not Daniel. "However, there is a God in heaven who reveals mysteries, and He has made known to King Nebuchadnezzar what will take place in the latter days" (Dan. 2:28). That must have seemed very strange to the king who was used to all his wise men, magicians, and sorcerers trumpeting their own skills of wisdom and divination. Here was a young man who gave all the credit to God.

Daniel not only held God as his personal hope, but he also proclaimed God to be the hope of all people. Later, Peter also stood firm in his faith and hope. "But sanctify Christ as Lord in your hearts, always being ready to make a defense to everyone who asks you to give an account for the hope that is in you, yet with gentleness and reverence" (1 Pet. 3:15). Daniel's gentleness and reverence in the proclamation of his hope is perhaps without parallel in scripture. There is no sense of derision or haughtiness in any of his dealings with his pagan bosses. He is a great example to us in all our dealings with both our fellow believers and those who have not found Jesus as their Lord and Savior.

Consider Daniel's plea with Nebuchadnezzar to change his ways. "Therefore, O king, may my advice be pleasing to you: break away now from your sins by *doing* righteousness and from your iniquities by showing mercy to *the* poor, in case there may be a prolonging of your prosperity" (Dan. 4:27). The fact that the king did not accept Daniel's plea is irrelevant to Daniel's faith. Daniel acted on the hope that was within him. The seed of truth was planted, God acted, and in the end the king proclaimed, "Now I, Nebuchadnezzar, praise, exalt and honor the King of heaven, for all His works are true and His ways just, and He is able to humble those who walk in pride" (Dan. 4:37).

It is with this hope that Daniel walked bravely into the lion's den. It was a hope he shared with his friends who walked bravely into the furnace. It was a hope manifested both in the miraculous and the mundane. It was a hope that did not rely on events or circumstances.

> *If it be so, our God whom we serve is able to deliver us from the furnace of blazing fire; and He will deliver us out of your hand, O king. But even if He does not, let it be known to you, O king, that we are not going to serve your gods or worship the golden image that you have set up.*

—Dan. 3:17–18

In the New Testament, the Apostle Paul held this hope even as he walked a path that he knew led to death.

> *For I am already being poured out as a drink offering, and the time of my departure has come. I have fought the good fight, I have finished the course, I have kept the faith; in the future there is laid up for me the crown of righteousness, which the Lord, the righteous Judge, will award to me on that day.*

—2 Tim. 4:6–8

Paul walked the hupomone path to martyrdom, giving his life. Daniel also walked the hupomone path, standing firm for the hope he had in God. In human terms, these two men had quite different ends, but before God, each of them lived the life of perseverance that He wants for all who call on His name.

Prayer

> *With all prayer and petition pray at all times in the Spirit, and with this in view, be on the alert with all perseverance and petition for all the saints, and pray on my behalf, that utterance may be given to me in the opening of my mouth, to make known with boldness the mystery of the gospel.*

—Eph. 6:18–19

The next aspect of hupomone that we see in Daniel's story is prayer. I really believe that Daniel and Paul are just chillin' together up in heaven, their lives mirroring many of the same qualities. Prayer is just one more of those qualities we see emphasized in both Paul and Daniel.

> *Now when Daniel knew that the document was signed, he entered his house (now in his roof chamber he had windows open toward Jerusalem); and he continued kneeling on his knees three times a day, praying and giving thanks before his God, as he had been doing previously.*

—Dan. 6:10

Prayer was important to Daniel. In fact, it was so important that the value he placed on it was clearly visible to all, even his enemies. When his enemies laid a trap by effectively outlawing prayer, Daniel risked everything to continue this vital communication with God. He had learned that connecting with God on a regular basis was key to his relationship with Him. Daniel was probably in his mid-60s by this time. I can only imagine how much he had learned the importance of prayer through his many years of experiences. Perhaps there had been times when the duties of his high administrative and political office had impacted his prayer life. There were probably times when he felt the spiritual staleness that comes when we let circumstances push God to the edges of our lives. He knew that no matter what, he had to spend time with God each and every day, regardless of the consequences.

Daniel valued prayer not only as a daily part of his life but also as a path to resolution for the concerns and problems that arose. He also valued the power of corporate prayer. He called on his godly companions to stand with him before the throne of God.

> *Then Daniel went to his house and informed his friends, Hananiah, Mishael and Azariah, about the matter, so that they might request compassion from the God of heaven concerning this mystery.*

—Dan. 2:17–18

Daniel is another great example of hupomone in his dedication to prayer, which was also at the heart of Jesus' ministry. We are given two wonderful, complete examples or models for prayer by our Lord and Savior in the Gospels. The first is, of course, the Lord's Prayer.

> *Pray, then, in this way:*
>
> *Our Father who is in heaven,*
> *Hallowed be Your name.*
> *Your kingdom come.*
> *Your will be done,*

> *On earth as it is in heaven.*
> *Give us this day our daily bread.*
> *And forgive us our debts, as we also have forgiven*
> *our debtors.*
> *And do not lead us into temptation, but deliver us*
> *from evil. [For Yours is the kingdom and the power*
> *and the glory forever. Amen.]*

—Matt. 6:9–13

The Gospel of John gives us a more comprehensive example of Jesus praying, not as a lesson but interceding before God for His children in John 17. Throughout the Gospels, Jesus makes prayer a salient aspect of His ministry. He spends extended times in prayer before important decisions or events. He withdraws from His active ministry repeatedly to spend time with His Father. Paul also understood the importance of prayer in securing rest, peace, and joy.

> *Rejoice in the Lord always; again, I will say, rejoice!*
> *Let your gentle* spirit *be known to all men. The Lord*
> *is near. Be anxious for nothing, but in everything by*
> *prayer and supplication with thanksgiving let your*
> *requests be made known to God. And the peace of*
> *God, which surpasses all comprehension, will guard*
> *your hearts and your minds in Christ Jesus.*

—Phil. 4:4–7

Prayer is not a requirement or a chore that must be accomplished daily to keep us in God's good graces. Paul certainly did not see it that way, and I do not believe Daniel did either. Prayer is a great privilege. For the hupomone man or woman who is in it with God for the long haul, prayer is a way of life.

Obedience

> *For you have need of endurance* [hupomone], *so that when you have done the will of God, you may receive what was promised.*

—Heb. 10:36

 Obedience is at the very core of perseverance. Obedience springs from our true hope in God and in the fact that He will do what He says He will do. Our hope springs from the obedience of our Savior.

> *For as through the one man's disobedience the many were made sinners, even so through the obedience of the One the many will be made righteous."*

—Rom. 5:19

Daniel understood obedience, as Paul did. He saw it as more than just the sum of our earthly actions; he saw it as a spiritual principle. In Daniel 1, we see a three-step process for biblical obedience.

Step 1: Choose

> *But Daniel made up his mind that he would not defile himself with the king's choice food or with the wine which he drank.*

—Dan. 1:8

The first step toward biblical obedience is of the heart and the mind. The King James Version of the Bible states, "Daniel purposed in his heart." The English Standard Version says, "Daniel resolved." The Hebrew here—*leb suwm*—is significant. *Leb* indicates a person's inner being. The root of the word is used of the people of Israel after the spies came back from the Promised Land. Ten delivered a report of fear, while Caleb and Joshua delivered a report of God. Moses stated, "Where can we go up? Our brethren have made our hearts melt, saying, 'The people are bigger and taller than we; the cities are large and fortified to heaven. And besides, we saw the sons of the Anakim there'" (Deut. 1:28).

Did you ever have a fear so intense that you felt like your innermost being was melting? Sometimes we call it "that sinking feeling." Moses went on to say, "But for all this, you did not trust the LORD your God, who goes before you on *your* way, to seek out a place for you to encamp, in fire by night and cloud by day, to show you the way in which you should go" (Deut. 1:32–33). The resolve to be obedient for the children of God (both New Testament and Old Testament) is tied up in our trust in the one true God, and it is that resolve that translates into biblical perseverance. Daniel directed his innermost core—through all his circumstances—not to defile himself before God.

Step 2: Relationships and Sharing

The second step in biblical obedience is relationships. Every one of us lives within a web of relationships that involves influence and authority. "So he sought *permission* from the commander of the officials that he might not defile himself" (Dan. 1:8). I think too often the people of God pursue obedience in arrogance. They use God as an excuse to ignore or defy authority in a disrespectful manner. Paul makes it clear what the relationship of a Jesus follower is to those in authority.

> *Every person is to be in subjection to the governing authorities. For there is no authority except from God, and those which exist are established by God. Therefore, whoever resists authority has opposed the ordinance of God; and they who have opposed will receive condemnation upon themselves.*

—Romans 13:1–2

Even when our faith requires us to obey God rather than men or women, we are to do it with respect and honor. Consider Daniel's three friends in the face of King Nebuchadnezzar's rage.

O Nebuchadnezzar, we do not need to give you an
answer concerning this matter. If it be so, our God
whom we serve is able to deliver us from the furnace
of blazing fire; and He will deliver us out of your
hand, O king. But even if He does *not, let it be*
known to you, O king, that we are not going to serve
your gods or worship the golden image that you
have set up.

—Dan. 3:16–18

Sharing is another aspect of perseverance in obedience. When hupomone is shared, it spreads. Not only did Daniel share his perseverance with the commander of officials, he also shared it with his friends. I can only imagine that this was one of the things the kings of Babylon appreciated in Daniel. As Daniel was obedient to God and persevered in his faith, perseverance multiplied in those around him, and with that multiplication, the blessings that came along with godly perseverance also multiplied. In that way, Daniel experienced incredible favor in a pagan land.

Step 3: Follow Through

Once we have chosen perseverance and shared it, we need to trust God as we follow through in our obedience. That is the part of obedience in perseverance where the rubber meets the road. It led James to say, "Even so faith, if it has no works, is dead, being by itself" (James 2:17). You can purpose in your heart and then share that all day long, but if your actions don't follow through with that purpose and those around you cannot match up what you are representing to them with what you are doing, then it is all a bunch of hooey.

Daniel and his friends engaged their purpose and sharing with real action that resulted in miraculous favor. I can only imagine that at first their actions were met with derision. As the other boys ate their sumptuous meals and drank the wine of the king's table, I am sure the obedience to this foreign god seemed pretty silly. When Daniel and his friends were elevated to high positions, it suddenly was not so funny. When God's people obey, the world notices.

Daniel's follow-through on his purpose and sharing was so consistent that his enemies knew that if they were going to bring him down, it would have to be by compromising his obedience to God. What they did not count on (or possibly believe in) was the miraculous intervention of Jehovah-Sabaoth, God our protector. Consider Jesus' words to His disciples.

> He said to His disciples, "It is inevitable that stumbling blocks come, but woe to him through whom they come! It would be better for him if a millstone were hung around his neck and he were thrown into the sea, than that he would cause one of these little ones to stumble."

—Luke 17:1–2

Daniel's enemies found that messing with his obedience to God had real consequences. Daniel portrays another aspect of persevering obedience in a story about his friends. When their stance on worshipping Nebuchadnezzar's golden idol on pain of death was challenged, this was their answer:

> *If it be so, our God whom we serve is able to deliver us from the furnace of blazing fire; and He will deliver us out of your hand, O king. But* even *if He does* not, *let it be known to you, O king, that we are not going to serve your gods or worship the golden image that you have set up.*

> —Dan. 3:17–18

Persevering obedience does not require a positive earthly outcome. The value of true obedience is spiritual and eternal. It is that kind of obedience that Jesus demonstrated as He moved through His earthly ministry toward the cross.

> *Being found in appearance as a man, He humbled Himself by becoming obedient to the point of death, even death on a cross. For this reason also, God highly exalted Him, and bestowed on Him the name which is above every name, so that at the name of Jesus every knee will bow, of those who are in heaven and on earth and under the earth, and that every tongue will confess that Jesus Christ is Lord, to the glory of God the Father.* —Phil. 2:8–11

Top 10 Reasons I Like Daniel

Reason #10
I live near Detroit, so I am used to the lions losing anyway.

Reason #9
Daniel was smart enough to be out of town when they stoked up the fiery furnace.

Reason #8
Daniel could actually say and spell Nebuchadnezzar correctly.

Reason #7
Daniel was a vegetarian...oh no...wait...yep, that is from the list of reasons *not* to like him.

Reason #6
Helen of Troy??? Whatever... angels and demons fought a war over him.

Reason #5
Daniel has the coolest *Veggie Tales* song ever.

Reason #4
Daniel did not get a dime of royalties from any of the diet and fasting plans that bear his name.

Reason #3
Daniel got the coolest Babylonian name. Who would not want to be called Belteshazzar?

Reason #2
Daniel is the only politician or civil servant who was quoted by Jesus.

And my #1 reason for liking Daniel
He was a true Hupomone Man, remaining "under God" as His servant through the rise and fall of kings and kingdoms.

Chapter 5

Strength, Bravery, and Weakness

> *Leadership strengths are often found in close proximity to blindspots. An overpowering strength, in particular, usually has an associated blindspot* (emphasis added).

> —Robert Bruce Shaw
> *Leadership Blindspots*

Strong Enough to Be Blind

I saw the above quote in one of the secular leadership blogs that come in my e-mail. I don't look closely at most of them anymore. However, this one caught my eye. I am always intrigued when a secular article espouses a biblical truth. I am certain that if you read Robert Bruce Shaw in depth, he differs considerably from the Apostle Paul's teachings.

> *And He has said to me, "My grace is sufficient for you, for power is perfected in weakness." Most gladly, therefore, I will rather boast about my weaknesses, so that the power of Christ may dwell in me.*

> —2 Cor. 12:9

In Philippians 3, Paul writes about what was becoming a huge blind spot for many of the Jewish believers. They had a strong belief in the overpowering strength of their

70

religious heritage. Paul's reply to this blind spot was that he, if anyone, had reason to rest in the strength of religious heritage. He went on to say:

> But whatever things were gain to me, those things I have counted as loss for the sake of Christ. More than that, I count all things to be loss in view of the surpassing value of knowing Christ Jesus my Lord, for whom I have suffered the loss of all things, and count them but rubbish so that I may gain Christ, and may be found in Him, not having a righteousness of my own derived from the Law, but that which is through faith in Christ, the righteousness which comes from God on the basis of faith, that I may know Him and the power of His resurrection and the fellowship of His sufferings, being conformed to His death.

—Phil. 3:7–10

These apparent strengths can even be gifts from God. Unfortunately, as Paul noted, the more overpowering the strength, the closer the blind spot. Consider Samson, called to save his people even before he was conceived and dedicated to God as a Nazirite from conception.

> Behold now, you are barren and have borne no children, but you shall conceive and give birth to a son. Now therefore, be careful not to drink wine or strong drink, nor eat any unclean thing. For behold, you shall conceive and give birth to a son, and no razor shall come upon his head, for the boy shall be a Nazirite to God from the womb ; and he shall

71

begin to deliver Israel from the hands of the
Philistines. —Judges 13:3–5

Samson had two great strengths. The most obvious one was his physical strength. The second was his godly discipline as a Nazirite. As the story unfolds, we see the blind spots that develop as he grows to be comfortable in his strengths. He achieves victory after victory, and as happens all too often, the blind spot involved a growing sense of power that self-eclipsed the very God who is the source and sustenance of that power. He ignored the godly counsel of his parents and then did not even seek wise counsel. After all, he was a Nazirite, the chosen one of God, who would counsel him.

Even when 3,000 men of Israel came to hand him over to the Philistines, Samson did not see the selfishness of his actions. He used the strengths given him by God out of anger and out of hurt, yet he continued his disciplines, and as promised, God set him as a judge over Israel. We so often equate success with righteousness. The Spirit of the Lord came upon Samson time after time, so he must have been in right relationship with God, right? That is a misconception that leads to great disappointment and injury. When men and women of God exercise their gifts in blind spots, God's will still moves through those strengths. But when they measure their fruit by Galatians 5, they see the disconnect. "But the fruit of the Spirit is love, joy, peace, patience, kindness, goodness, faithfulness, gentleness, self-control; against such things there is no law" (Gal. 5:22–23).

Here are the issues that point to the blind spots Samson fostered and ignored:

- His disregard for his parents
- His failure to seek godly and wise counsel as his mother had done. "Then Manoah entreated the LORD and said, 'O Lord, please let the man of God whom You have sent come to us again that he may teach us what to do for the boy who is to be born'" (Judges 13:8).
- His lack of concern for the consequences of his actions on the very people he was sent to save

While scripture does not record it, Samson's parents most likely constantly and desperately attempted to reach their son. Wise counsel, whether it is from parents, mentors, or just people God places in our lives, is key in order to illuminate the blind spots the enemy will manipulate to harm us and those around us. Samson is a good example of blind spots because in the end, it brought him physical blindness. The will of God for his life was ultimately achieved as he brought the house down on the Philistines and their power in the region. But how much more of a story it would have been if his blind spots had not brought such tragedy and interrupted God's call on his life.

Pondering Bravery – Allana

"So here I sit, pondering bravery," Allana once wrote. "What does it truly mean to be brave?" Allana always greatly enjoyed reading devotionals. She said all too often, "Yep, me too." There always seems to be a little nugget that she took away. Morning after morning, she would sit there listening to the children clicking away on their computers doing their schoolwork. She listened to her mom busily cleaning, and she listened to Nisa Faith's giggles. She would ask herself, "What does it mean to be brave? Who are my heroes of faith?" Each day she had a different answer and a different way to explain why their actions were brave. But she always said they had one thing in common. They were human. Yep, they were imperfect humans. Well, we can do *that*, right?

Allana often recalled the story of Beth Moore. If you have never heard or read her story about the hairbrush, you should google it. It is an amazing act of bravery. But what Allana loved most about the story was how incredibly human Beth was. I think so often about how we raise people up much higher than they should be. Many times, Allana felt people do that to her. We look up to them, she would say, and they seem to have it all together. But do you want to know something? No one truly has it all together. We are all walking a road. No one walks their road perfectly—none but Jesus.

We sometimes struggle with fear—paralyzing fear that at times robs us of peace. But there are also flashes of brave moments that come pouring through our lives. It is time to stop getting hung up on our human moments. We need to start looking through God-glasses and start accepting who He says we are. We often go through a long list of how we are not brave, but being brave doesn't mean we don't have fear. We can be brave and still be afraid.

Allana had gone through one of her most difficult rounds of chemo. She was extremely sick, wondering if she would live to see another day, wondering if I would ever kiss her forehead again, wondering if she would ever have another deep talk with her teenagers, wondering if she would be there to kiss her preteen's hurt away, wondering if her newborn baby would have her as her mother. She would lie in bed crying out from her heart for God to help her. And she thought about Jesus calming the sea.

> And there arose a fierce gale of wind, and the waves were breaking over the boat so much that the boat was already filling up. Jesus Himself was in the stern, asleep on the cushion; and they woke Him and said to Him, "Teacher, do You not care that we are perishing?" And He got up and rebuked the wind and said to the sea, "Hush, be still." And the wind died down and it became perfectly calm.
>
> —Mark 4:37–39

Allana begged God to calm her sea. And then she remembered another story, much like this one only with a twist.

> Immediately He made the disciples get into the boat and go ahead of Him to the other side, while He sent the crowds away. After He had sent the crowds away, He went up on the mountain by Himself to pray; and when it was evening, He was there alone. But the boat was already a long distance

from the land, battered by the waves; for the wind was contrary. And in the fourth watch of the night He came to them, walking on the sea. When the disciples saw Him walking on the sea, they were terrified, and said, "It is a ghost!" And they cried out in fear. But immediately Jesus spoke to them, saying, "Take courage, it is I; do not be afraid."

Peter said to Him, "Lord, if it is You, command me to come to You on the water." And He said, "Come!" And Peter got out of the boat, and walked on the water and came toward Jesus. But seeing the wind, he became frightened, and beginning to sink, he cried out, "Lord, save me!" Immediately Jesus stretched out His hand and took hold of him, and said to him, "You of little faith, why did you doubt?" When they got into the boat, the wind stopped.

—Matt. 14:22–32

Did you see it? Jesus called Peter out of the boat with the waves crashing around him. Jesus did not calm the sea first. The wind died down when they climbed back into the boat. Jesus touched Allana's heart with this passage and told her, "I am the God who will calm your sea, but I am also the God who will have you step out in your storm." That was a moment that Jesus encouraged Allana's heart to be brave. God may calm your storm, or He may call you out of the boat while the waves are still crashing around you. But regardless, He is always there to catch you.

Weak Enough to See

And he was three days without sight, and neither ate nor drank.

—Acts 9:9

This verse comes from a story that many of us may know well. It is the conversion story of Saul, who would become Paul the Apostle. Paul was a man who acutely understood the dangers of blind spots; Saul was not. Saul, along with many of the Jewish leaders of his day, lived in a big blind spot. They desperately believed in God and in the coming Messiah, but they saw their heritage and tradition as an overwhelming strength. In that feeling of strength, they were blind to the truth of the gospel. Saul in his strength attended and approved of the stoning of Stephen. He even watched over the cloaks of the men involved (Acts 7:58–8:1). Saul in his strength, "still breathing threats and murder against the disciples of the Lord" (Acts 9:1), sought the destruction of the early Church. He is an ominous example of this: When we attempt to serve God in the strength of tradition, skill, knowledge, or any other personal trait, the greater our service, the greater our potential blind spot.

So then, this is the question: How do we avoid operating in spiritual blind spots? Prior to committing our lives to the Lord Jesus Christ, we lived in darkness. It is a way of life for those who are not in a personal relationship with Him. Jesus came to take us from the darkness that is life without God and bring us into the light.

I have come as Light into the world, so that everyone who believes in Me will not remain in darkness.

—John 12:46

Old habits die hard, and Peter, speaking to believers, sheds light on spiritual blind spots.

For by these He has granted to us His precious and magnificent promises, so that by them you may become partakers of the divine nature, having escaped the corruption that is in the world by lust. Now for this very reason also, applying all diligence, in your faith supply moral excellence, and in your moral excellence, knowledge, and in your knowledge, self-control, and in your self-control, perseverance, and in your perseverance, godliness, and in your godliness, brotherly kindness, and in your brotherly kindness, love. For if these qualities are yours and are increasing, they render you neither useless nor unfruitful in the true knowledge of our Lord Jesus Christ. For he who lacks these qualities is blind or short-sighted, having forgotten his purification from his former sins.

—2 Pet. 1:4–9

We can compare this passage to Paul's exposition on the fruit of the Spirit in Galatians 5. These passages and many like them provide a spiritual litmus test for smoking out blind spots in our walk with God. However, I want to go back to Paul's story to see how God dealt with this problem in his life.

1. God knocked Saul from his high horse.

   As he was traveling, it happened that he was approaching Damascus, and suddenly a light from heaven flashed around him; and he fell to the ground.

   —Acts 9:3–4

2. God brought Saul to a place of weakness.

   a. Paul was blinded. The spiritual state he was operating in was manifested physically.

   b. The man who was accustomed to leading needed to be led into the city.

   c. Paul was unable to eat or drink for three days.

3. God spoke truth into Saul's life.

   a. Initially, God spoke directly to Saul, revealing the blind spot he was operating under.

   b. God revealed Saul's personal inadequacy in a vision of the man who would come to help him.

   c. God brought a Christian brother to speak healing into Saul's life, both physical and Spiritual blindness.

Fortunately, God has provided us with scripture, including Paul's example and the examples of many other men and women of God throughout biblical history. With the help of the Holy Spirit, we can smoke out our blind spots without being knocked off a horse and blinded.

1. Examine ourselves for areas of personal (denominational, doctrinal, etc.) pride that can make us susceptible to blind spots. Then we need to follow Micah's advice: "He has told you, O man, what is good; and what does the LORD require of you but to do justice, to love kindness, and to walk humbly with your God?" (Micah 6:8).
2. Do not be afraid to operate from areas of weakness or in positions of weakness.
3. Always be ready for, looking for, and expecting the truth of God to be revealed in your life. The primary source is, of course, scripture. The more time you spend in scripture with your heart and mind open to God's message, the less likely you are to function in a blind spot. And always walk with solid brothers and sisters in Christ who will be honest and open with you. God may or may not reveal them to you in a vision, but be ready to listen to the Holy Spirit as He speaks through them. Filter it all through the truth of scripture.

Blind spots are endemic to our human nature, but God through the work of Jesus Christ and the gift of the Holy Spirit as recorded in scripture has provided us all with the tools to walk in the light as the children of God.

Chapter 6

Lessons in Hope

For in hope we have been saved, but hope that is seen is not hope; for who hopes for what he already *sees? But if we hope for what we do not see, with perseverance we wait eagerly for it.*

—Romans 8:24–25

I wrestled with the eighth chapter of Romans for weeks. In fact, I am still struggling with it and will probably continue to struggle with it. The chapter is not meant to be doctrine or even counsel. It is simply emotional and spiritual transparency from a moment when God spoke into my life.

Some time ago, real hope with perseverance sat next to me. He probably does not even realize how profoundly he impacted my life. God is so amazing in the way He pairs the events of our lives with biblical truths He lays on our hearts. This man and his loved ones walked the path of cancer that Allana and I, along with our family, walked. He rode the roller coaster of emotion. He even walked the same hospital hallways. He prayed and was prayed for. He held those he loved and was held by them. A few short weeks before I met him, a vibrant woman of God, his beloved wife, died. I will only meet her when I get to stand in the presence of my God.

As I sat there with my lovely Allana across from me, God whispered in my ear—okay, maybe He shouted. **"Is this the sum of all your fears or the truth of all your hope?"**

> *But if we hope for what we do not see, with perseverance we wait eagerly for it."*

—Rom. 8:25

Hope and perseverance are inexorably entwined for the believer. It is not hope in the visible and perseverance in the seen; it is a hope that is embedded in faith.

> *Now faith is the assurance of* things *hoped for, the conviction of things not seen.*

—Hebrews 11:1

All the numbers I had heard and read rolled through my mind—all percentages of life and death, grief and fear walking alongside faith and hope as I stood with my beloved. They were the same grief, fear, faith, and hope I saw sitting next to me. **"Is this the sum of all your fears or the truth of all your hope?"**

Saturday: Hupomone Day

We celebrate Good Friday. We celebrate Easter. What about Saturday?

Sandwiched between the suffering of the greatest sacrifice ever made and the glory of the most magnificent triumph ever won—past, present, or future—is *what*? I am going to call it Hupomone Day because it is the Saturdays of our life that grow true perseverance.

How often do we find ourselves on Saturday—that blank day between the suffering and the triumph? At least as we watch the events unfold, we can focus on the horror and the pain. We can anticipate the miraculous escape, the triumphant turning of the tide as God magnificently brings the victory. Then it does not happen the way we want or expect. The night falls—a restless night, perhaps without sleep, certainly with disturbed dreams. Then what about Saturday? What do we do? Dawn comes, but all we see is Friday's darkness. The birds are singing, but all we can hear are the screams and jeers of the crowd, the hammering of the nails, the moans of Jesus' mother, the pounding of our own heart.

What about Saturday? What do we do? What should we do? Some will run. Some will hide. Some will lose faith and return to the life they knew before they felt the Master's touch. Some will struggle and doubt.

struggle and doubt + faith = hupomone

Now faith is the assurance of things *hoped for, the conviction of things not seen.*

—Heb. 11:1

Some of us have longer Saturdays than others. Take Thomas. I often hear people make fun of doubting Thomas. I can only imagine that his fellow disciples gave him some ribbing, but here is the deal. Thomas stayed! He made it through a Saturday that was longer and more intense than any of the others. I can only believe that Saturday made his Sunday morning even more amazing. Thomas grew through his Saturday. He walked away with an understanding of Hebrews 11:1 straight from the lips of his Savior:

> *Jesus said to him, "Because you have seen Me, have you believed? Blessed* are they *who did not see, and yet believed."*

—John 20:29

If Friday is Good Friday and Sunday is Easter Sunday, then Saturday is Hupomone Saturday. Saturday is when we remember His Word. Saturday is when we remember His touch. On Saturday, the fellowship of our brothers and sisters in Christ becomes paramount. On Saturday, we scream out to God. On Saturday, we worship, we cry, we hurt, we heal—in spite of ourselves. On Saturday, we grow and mature as on no other day. Perhaps that is why Saturday is in God's plan for us. I have experienced a few Saturdays in my life. Some I am still experiencing. While

Sunday mornings are great, it is the Saturdays that draw me close to God and close to God's people.

It is on Saturday that I make strides toward Philippians 2, learning humility and allowing God to work in me. It is on Saturday that God makes those subtle changes in me that draw my spirit, soul, and body closer to having His attitude and His values and to truly having His love.

It is on Saturday that we practice Hebrews 11:1 like no other day. Do we trust the promise? Are we certain of our hope? It is on Saturday that we, along with Joshua, say amid it all, "As for me and my house, we will serve the LORD" (Josh. 24:15).

Unfortunately, I think it is also on Saturday that all too many lose faith, not able to hold on to the promise. It is on Saturday as on no other day that brothers and sisters in Christ fail each other. Perhaps it is because we do not realize that every day is someone's Saturday.

> *Bear one another's burdens, and thereby fulfill the law of Christ.*

> —Gal. 6:2

Are you in the midst of Saturday? Be certain that Sunday morning is coming. And when it does, the most miraculous thing—the most miraculous change—will not be the situation you are experiencing. It will be YOU!

Hupomone Sniffed Out

I was driving down a local road on my way home recently when I passed a car that a Toledo police officer had pulled over. Just as I passed them, the officer opened the back door of his cruiser and let out a police dog. My view then turned to the young lady in the driver's seat. I caught her just as she became aware of the impending visit by the police dog. Her face was a mixture of fear, guilt, regret, and despair. That moment captured a whole series of decisions that had led her to this moment.

I could not help thinking that right then she personified the plight of humanity in the face of a righteous God. She was Adam and Eve hiding in the garden from the voice of God (Gen. 3:8). She was the mass of humanity pounding on the door of the Ark (Gen. 7:21). She was David standing before Nathan the prophet (2 Sam. 12). She was Ananias and Sapphira standing before Peter (Acts 5). The implications of her plight did not approach the consequences in each of these biblical examples, but I can only imagine that her heart was very much in the same place. I cannot speak to her knowledge of God or to the potential relationships that have spoken truth to her. And I will probably never know the final consequences of this moment in her life.

This is a moment we have all experienced. We have all had those "sniffed out" moments. We look in the mirror and see the dog that will sniff out our dishonesty, our greed, our anger, our sin and make its way toward the vehicle of our life. Our hearts experience the same mix of emotion that I saw on our unnamed young lady's face. What I could not see and what makes all the difference is what her soul (and ours) does with the emotions of being sniffed out.

Sin is universal and an unavoidable result of the human condition (Rom. 3:23). The Holy Spirit is the ultimate "police dog," perfect in His ability to sniff out and expose sin (John 16:7–10). The big difference is that the Holy Spirit desperately loves the sinner (John 3:16). When the Holy Spirit sniffs out sin, He wraps us in His arms and does His best to lead us to repentance and redemption. God sacrificed His Son Jesus Christ to ensure this could happen. We only have to reach out to Him and "take the deal." When we take it, the sentence is an eternity of praising God in perfect relationship with Him. It is a deal that cannot be scammed, tricked, or manipulated. There is no negotiation. It is the ultimate deal offered by the one true God. There is only one alternative—death (Rom. 6:23).

God calls us to focus on the gospel, the good news, when the Holy Spirit convicts. Hopelessness and terror are the message of the devil. He works to turn the work of the Holy Spirit into condemnation and despair. Paul recognized this when he penned one of my favorite chapters in the Bible, Romans 8.

> *Therefore, there is now no condemnation for those who are in Christ Jesus. For the law of the Spirit of life in Christ Jesus has set you from the law of sin and of death.*

> —Rom. 8:1–2

It is Satan's greatest desire that we suffer fear, the despair of the Law, twisting the loving act of conviction into the hateful act of condemnation. Paul goes on to speak of this very Holy Spirit that sniffs out our sin.

> For you have not received a spirit of slavery leading to fear again, but you have received a spirit of adoption as sons by which we cry out, "Abba! Father!"

—Rom. 8:15

Imagine with me for a moment that even as that police dog sniffs out the young woman's sin, she throws her arms around his neck, confessing her own blindness, and lets him lead her out of despair into the light of adoption, a light brighter and more full of hope than the lights of a thousand police cars. This is the very beginning of hupomone. It is the moment when we recognize the shifting sands of our own lives and choose to step up onto the Rock.

Chapter 7

Major Endurance

Trust in the Lord *forever,*
For in God the Lord, *we have an everlasting Rock.*

—Isaiah 26:4

Called

The prophets of the Old Testament often highlighted the lack of hupomone in the lives of those around them. However, more important than that was their spiritual character. Isaiah and Jeremiah—those guys were some major Hupomone Men! Depending on how you figure the history and do the math, Isaiah spoke for God over a period of around 60 years. Jeremiah's career spanned about 40 years. They were both fearless before men and absolutely devoted to God. They were both despised and revered. They were both threatened and abused for their devotion to the word of the Lord. They were both honored by recognition in the New Testament. Jeremiah is even called out as a potential identity for Jesus Christ. Isaiah is recognized as the most prolific messianic prophet. He foretold John the Baptist and his mission. It was the book of Isaiah that the Ethiopian eunuch was reading on his way home from Jerusalem.

So what is it about these two men that makes them truly hupomone men?

Isaiah and Jeremiah were both called by God to serve Him and speak to the people for Him.

> *Before I formed you in the womb I knew you,*
> *And before you were born I consecrated you;*
> *I have appointed you a prophet to the nations.*

—Jer. 1:5

> *Then I heard the voice of the Lord, saying, "Whom shall I send, and who will go for Us?" Then I said, "Here am I. Send me!"*

—Isa. 6:8

The call of God on our lives is at the very core of hupomone. There is an illusion here that can trip us up. It may appear to us that the call of God on the lives of Jeremiah and Isaiah was about being a prophet. The book of Jeremiah is a little more explicit about the nature of God's call on Jeremiah's life. While the call extends to vocation, it is not at its center about vocation. "And before you were born I consecrated you" (Jer. 1:5). Jeremiah was set apart to be in relationship with God long before he ever delivered a word from God. With the words, "Here am I. Send me!" Isaiah is already positioned to hear the voice of God before he seals his vocation.

Paul lays out the course of hupomone for a young pastor named Timothy.

> *Who has saved us and called us with a holy calling,*
> *not according to our works, but according to His*
> *own purpose and grace which was granted us in*
> *Christ Jesus from all eternity.*

> —2 Tim. 1:9

Hupomone begins with salvation. It is only when we accept the extended hand of fellowship from God, which includes a call to be separated and holy, that we open the door to the steadfast, enduring lifestyle of abandoning our own purposes to follow God's. Paul makes it clear that this call is not about anything we have done (or by extension anything Isaiah or Jeremiah had done). It is an undeserved gift. It is grace. In Ephesians, Paul tells us that the very nature of this calling gives us hope.

> I pray that *the eyes of your heart may be*
> *enlightened, so that you will know what is the hope*
> *of His calling, what are the riches of the glory of His*
> *inheritance in the saints.*

> —Eph. 1:18

The kind of perseverance we see rising out of the call of God comes about from having a view to eternity and to the inheritance of the saints, first to Israel in the Old Testament and then opened up to all humankind by the death and resurrection of our Lord and Savior Jesus Christ.

Daily

Trust in the LORD forever,
For in God the LORD, we have an everlasting Rock.

If you have followed me for long, you realize that I have a hupomone fetish. The word is just cool. As I was reading the books of Isaiah and Jeremiah, I kept hearing this over and over: "These guys are real Hupomone Men." Yes, when I read scripture, I often hear things, and no, it is not always God. Sometimes it is something like, "There is ice cream in the freezer." But when I read about Isaiah and Jeremiah, I focus not so much on the message that these two great prophets delivered but on the lives they lived. The message made them prophets of God. Their lives made them men of God—Hupomone Men.

In the previous section of this chapter, we established that Isaiah and Jeremiah were Hupomone Men because they were called by God. You may be thinking, "Well, that lets me off the hook. I am not called to be a prophet!" The Romans may have been thinking the same thing when Paul disabused them of that idea by opening the epistle to the believers in Rome with this:

Jesus Christ our Lord, through whom we have received grace and apostleship to bring about the *obedience of faith among all the Gentiles for His name's sake, among whom **you** also are the called of Jesus Christ; to **all** who are beloved of God in Rome, **called** as saints: Grace to you and peace from*

God our Father and the Lord Jesus Christ (emphasis added).

—Rom. 1:4–7

Yes, we are not all called to be prophets, but we are called to obedience, called to sainthood—*hagios*, which comes from a root that indicates purity and freedom from sin. This call for Jeremiah and Isaiah took on its face the prophetic, serving an Israel that had lost its way. This call may be quite different for each person reading this book. The call is not to a specific vocation but to "the obedience of faith" (Rom. 8:5). Jesus makes it clear that the call is not enough. In his parable of the wedding guests, he concludes, "For many are called, but few *are* chosen" (Matt. 22:14).

As we look at the story (and I am not going to recount the whole thing here, so grab your Bible and read it), we see that the hapless guest to whom Jesus refers was called to the party but behaved himself out of being chosen to stay. This is where we see that the call is not enough. So what is this other thing, this next step that sets Isaiah and Jeremiah and all those Hupomone Men before and after them apart from the crowd?

> *If it is disagreeable in your sight to serve the* LORD, *choose for yourselves today whom you will serve: whether the gods which your fathers served which were beyond the River, or the gods of the Amorites in whose land you are living; but as for me and my house, we will serve the* LORD.

—Josh. 24:15

Joshua in his famous soliloquy before the people of Israel said to "choose for yourselves today." Isaiah and Jeremiah had many "todays" in their combined 100 years of prophetic service to God. There is another quality that set them apart as true Hupomone Men.

Isaiah and Jeremiah both made a daily choice to serve God.

They came dressed in their wedding clothes day after day. Even when all the other prophets were sporting Bermuda shorts and Hawaiian shirts, they came in wedding clothes. Even when the king made it clear that the honeymoon was over, they came in wedding clothes. And while scripture does not record it, tradition tells us that even when it meant death, they came in wedding clothes. They wore wedding clothes of obedience, truth, and purity. They wore the wedding clothes of the Hupomone Man.

Love

We are looking at some of the qualities of Isaiah and Jeremiah that contributed to their incredible endurance as men of God. They are qualities that qualify them to be wonderful examples of Hupomone Men. These qualities are not a function of their vocation as prophets of God. These qualities are not tied up in the message that Isaiah and Jeremiah brought to the people of God. These qualities are all about the daily choices of life that Isaiah and Jeremiah made as they responded to the call of God to be in relationship with Him. The quality of hupomone we are going to look at is a direct result of that relationship.

The LORD appeared to him from afar, saying,
"I have loved you with an everlasting love;
Therefore I have drawn you with lovingkindness."

—Jer. 31:3

Isaiah and Jeremiah had every reason to hate God's people. Given the content of many of their prophesies (particularly Jeremiah), we might settle on the idea that they did, indeed, hate. Here in the United States, we as a society have embraced the idea of "thought correctness," which violates the very core of hupomone love. The idea is that if you hate a behavior I am involved in, you hate me. That idea rejects the intrinsic value of the individual, the very basis of God's love for us. It limits the value of a person to their actions. God cries out to His people that He hates their behavior and its consequences but loves them with an everlasting love. The New Testament word for this kind of love is *agape*. It is the love that is the foundation of hupomone living. The call emanates from God to our spiritual ears and is a function of listening. It is Jesus' cry: "He who has ears to hear, let him hear" (Matt. 11:15). Daily choice is a function of will. It is the physical response to truly hearing God. Love is a function of relationship. It is the foundation that enables all the rest of it.

If I speak with the tongues of men and of angels,
but do not have love, I have become a noisy gong or
a clanging cymbal.

—1 Cor. 13:1

Isaiah and Jeremiah desperately and completely loved God. They desperately and completely loved God's people. It was this love extending from their relationship with God that drove their hupomone lifestyle for a combined 100 years. Faithfully they spoke truth to Israel, often reaping derision and persecution, but it was *agape* that validated their ministry. Some look at the prophets of the Old Testament and see hate and condemnation. I look and see hupomone living. I see the call of God to live out His everlasting love daily through meaningful choices empowered by the Holy Spirit. I see the great provision of grace seeking to redeem the results of rebellion. I hear God calling out through His people the message of love, redemption, and hupomone.

Purpose

Ezekiel was one far-out dude. I could focus on the wheels, sing about "dem dry bones," or wish I could see the beasts of his prophecy in the zoo, but I want to step away from the details of Ezekiel's message. Let's focus on an aspect of Ezekiel's life that makes him another Hupomone Man.

Ezekiel was from a priestly family, and, like Daniel, he was taken from his home in Israel and brought to Babylon. His family was probably prominent and influential. Bible scholar Charles Ryrie places him among the many hostages that Nebuchadnezzar took to ensure the cooperation of his newly conquered land. Unlike Isaiah and Jeremiah, Ezekiel prophesied to the Jews in Babylon.

As I read through the book of Ezekiel this time around, I really tried not to focus on the words of the prophecies given to him by God. I did not want to get caught up in the wonder and beautiful detail of Ezekiel's dreams. I really wanted to get a feel for Ezekiel the man. That is perhaps most difficult to do with Ezekiel—one of those we call the Major Prophets—since there is minimal historical detail. With the details out of focus, I began noticing this recurring phrase: "and you will know that I am the LORD" (Ezek. 37:6). The Holy Spirit whispered in my ear, "Hupomone Men have purpose." Honestly, it took me a bit to make the connection (I probably could have used Ezekiel's help—connecting the bones of my thoughts together—okay, ouch! That was bad).

Ezekiel completely understood the purpose of everything he said and did. Speaking for God was not an abstract activity. The life of the Hupomone Man is not an abstract activity. It has purpose. It really has one overarching purpose—to act, speak, write, and live in such a way that those around you can "know that He is the Lord." Peter put it this way:

> *Whoever speaks,* is to do so *as one who is speaking the utterances of God; whoever serves* is to do so *as one who is serving by the strength which God supplies, so that in all things God may be glorified through Jesus Christ, to whom belongs the glory and dominion forever and ever. Amen.*

> —1 Pet. 4:11

As Hupomone Men or Women, we can be sure that everything that happens in our lives is somehow contributing to this purpose, either for ourselves or for those around us. Ezekiel deeply understood this. Even as his wife passed away, there was purpose. This is all part of our great assurance that God is in control. We cannot, we must not allow circumstances to impinge on this great peace that we have as children of God. Ezekiel never lost sight of his purpose through all the turmoil, through all the circumstances of his life. He demonstrated major endurance and certainly earned the title Hupomone Man.

The Delight of Your Eyes

> *Son of man, behold, I am about to take from you the desire of your eyes with a blow; but you shall not mourn and you shall not weep, and your tears shall not come.*
>
> —Ezek. 24:16

Serving God can at times be overwhelming. We are not told a lot about Ezekiel's wife, just that she was the delight of his eyes. Ezekiel loved her. She was perhaps, next to God, the most important thing in Ezekiel's life. I have heard it taught that Ezekiel somehow sinned in his desire for his wife, that he had placed her above his devotion to God. That is simply not in the text and perhaps arises from the desire to believe that God is here to serve us instead of the other way around. We serve a God who loves us immensely. We also serve a God who commands ultimate obedience, honor, and trust. The circumstances surrounding this loss are not known to us. It can be supposed that Ezekiel's wife succumbed to a fatal illness, a much more common occurrence in those days than living a long and healthy life. Having been there many times for Allana, I can easily imagine Ezekiel crying out to God in prayer over her. I cannot but believe that Ezekiel's wife was a godly woman, the respected and honored wife of a priest. Why, O Lord, does she have to go through this? And the answer came: "For my purposes."

Paul understood service to God when he wrote to the Philippians, "For to you it has been *granted* for Christ's sake, not only to believe in Him, but also to suffer for His sake" (emphasis added) (Phil. 1:29). The word *carizomai* (translated *granted*) does not mean imposed upon or required. It carries the sense of a pleasant task, a favor, something given benevolently. As God's servants, suffering for His name and for His purposes is part of the gift, but we find that this gift is also paired with something else.

> *Rejoice in the Lord always; again I will say, rejoice!*
> *Let your gentle* spirit *be known to all men.*
> *The Lord is near. Be anxious for nothing, but in everything by prayer and supplication with thanksgi ving let your requests be made known to God.*
> *And the peace of God,*
> *which surpasses all comprehension, will*
> *guard your hearts and your minds in Christ Jesus.*

> —Phil. 4:4–7

This does not mean that everything is going to go the way we desire; it means that through the storm we will be able to say, "It is well with my soul."

God called Ezekiel to more than just losing the love of his life. He was called to contravene the social norms of the day and not enter into what was the common practice of very public and very loud mourning. God called him to "groan silently" (Ezek. 24:17). Paul says, "Let your gentle *spirit* be known to all men" (Phil. 4:5). We are called to a holy standard not only in the gift of suffering for His name but also in the Holy Spirit empowered ability to break the customs of this world in our reaction to that suffering and show the very nature of God in our actions. When we do that, the world takes notice.

> *And in the evening my wife died. And in*
> *the morning, I did as I was commanded. The people*
> *said to me, "Will you not tell us what*
> *these things that you are doing mean for us?*

—Ezek. 24:18–19

It is in the very city of Philippi that we get the story of the Philippian jailer. After being beaten and praising God through a night of imprisonment, Paul and Silas led their captive audience, the jailer, and his whole family to Jesus. The jailer asked them, "Sirs, what must I do to be saved?" (Acts 16:30).

The Abundant Life

> *The thief comes only to steal and kill and destroy; I came that they may have life, and have it abundantly.*

—John 10:10

So far, we have talked about characteristics of some men we call the Major Prophets, characteristics that qualify them as Hupomone Men. They were all called by God to be His (just as we are). They all committed their way to Him in body, mind, and soul—and perhaps more importantly, in their daily actions. They recognized and imitated God's undying love for a disobedient people. Finally, their core purpose was to serve God, even when it meant death.

We might be tempted to think that the hupomone life is a horrible grind. We may even take the attitude that life is horrible, but as people of God, we will endure it. There have been (and are) entire movements of faith based on this very concept, that somehow our lives as people of God should be slogging through a swamp of suffering. That is not the lot of the Hupomone Man or Woman. It is the abundant life, as the above scripture makes very clear. But the Hupomone Man or Woman is also going to walk through life with some negative circumstances.

Daniel survived the siege of Jerusalem. He was ripped from his family and taken to Babylon to serve the very man who destroyed his home. Every move Daniel made and recorded

101

for us reflects the Hupomone Man and the abundant life God affords to those who follow Him. It is an abundance that is not dependent on circumstances. It is an abundance born of patience, of perseverance. It is an abundance that causes three young men to face a mighty king and say, "Our God whom we serve is able to deliver us from the furnace of blazing fire; and He will deliver us out of your hand, O king. But *even* if *He does* not, let it be known to you, O king, that we are not going to serve your gods or worship the golden image that you have set up" (Dan. 3:17–18). Daniel faced the lion's den with the aplomb of someone who recognized the abundance of the hupomone life. It is an abundance that transcends death itself. It is a life that is based on the very Word of God.

> *All Scripture is inspired by God and profitable for teaching, for reproof, for correction, for training in righteousness; so that the man of God may be adequate, equipped for good work.*

> —2 Tim. 3:16–17

Paul called on all followers of Christ to live the hupomone life. It is a life that does not depend on circumstances but is anchored firmly on the Rock, Jesus Christ our Lord and Savior.

> *But you, be sober in all things, endure hardship, do the work of an evangelist, fulfill your ministry.*

> —2 Tim. 4:5

And not only this, but we also exult in our tribulations, knowing that tribulation brings about perseverance; and perseverance, proven character; and proven character, hope; and hope does not disappoint, because the love of God has been poured out within our hearts through the Holy Spirit who was given to us.

—Rom. 5:3–5

The Hupomone Man or Woman has enveloped themselves in the hope that does not disappoint. Peter calls it "a living hope" (1 Pet. 1:3). It is this hope that is the basis of the abundant life we have in Jesus, and it is at the core of hupomone living.

The Tale of Two Temples

When we think of the Old Testament Temple, most of us think of Solomon in all his glory. Solomon, the son of King David, is usually recognized as the greatest king of the Jewish people. He was rich beyond measure, was recognized for his wisdom, and had incredible international influence. He reigned over an unprecedented era of peace for Israel.

Solomon was called upon by God to build the Temple to house the Ark of the Covenant and God's revealed presence in Israel. Solomon was able to call upon the best of the best artisans and use the best materials in the known world. Gifts poured in from all over to help complete this monumental task. 1 Kings 5–7 provides us with the glorious details of this building, which was like no other in history. The author of 1 Kings provides us with wonderful detail about the construction and furnishings that defined this wonderful project. All the wealth and influence God provided to Solomon was represented in Solomon's obedience to this command of God.

There is another Temple builder in the Old Testament. He is less known, and most likely no one is named after him. He did not have the wealth, the fame, or the influence that Solomon had during the building of the first Temple. Zerubbabel was returning to Judah, which was less than half of the kingdom Solomon ruled. He was returning to a land that had been laid waste by Nebuchadnezzar, a land and a people that had suffered the consequences of rebellion both against God and against Babylon. Zerubbabel returned to Jerusalem with a ragtag group of exiles who had been born and raised in a foreign land. He came from the line of David, but he was not really a king. He had ruled at the pleasure of Babylon, and the land he governed was more of a province than a kingdom. He was surrounded by adversaries, not allies. Zerubbabel did not command the immense respect given to Solomon. Biblically, he takes a back seat to Ezra and even to Cyrus, King of Persia. Even after he completed the Temple, it was not all pats on the back and cheers. There were also jeers in the crowd. The few who were old enough to remember the former glory of the Temple built by Solomon decried this new Temple as inadequate. Yet through all this, Zerubbabel ruled over an incredible revival in Judah.

Comparison is one the greater weapons Satan uses to undermine the faith of the Hupomone Man or Woman. Here we have two men, both called to the same task, one from a position of wealth, strength, and glory and the other from a place of defeat, servitude, and subjection. Zerubbabel could have fallen into a rut of rebellious comparison and said, "But God, you gave Solomon everything to build your Temple, and I have nothing. I am not even really a king." We are so tempted to view the path that God has lain before us in comparison to others who seem to have it all. Sometimes we even compare our current call to a place where we were before. Paul understood this risky place well when he penned these words:

> I know how to get along with humble means, and I also know how to live in prosperity; in any and every circumstances I have learned the secret of being filled and growing hungry, both of having abundance and suffering need. I can do all things through Him who strengthens me.

> —Phil. 4:12–13

This is the position of the Hupomone Man or Woman. They see the nature of obedience resting not in the arms of ever-changing circumstances but in the arms of an unchanging God. We do not know a lot of details about Zerubbabel, but this son of a son of exile did not shirk his duty to serve YAWEH. He obeyed the call of God on his life and was true to his position as a son of David, even when faced with opposition that compared his humble state to the glory days of Israel. Though relegated to the closet of history, he stands as an example of a Hupomone Man that we would do well to follow.

Fan into Flame the Gift

> *For this reason, I remind you to fan into flame the gift of God, which is in you through the laying on of my hands.*

> —2 Tim. 1:6 NIV

God spoke this verse to Allana and me back in 2003. We had only been together a couple of years. They were difficult years. Allana had to adjust to being married, raising John, Robert, and Samantha—the three children who had completed our marriage and made us an instant family— and caring for our then newborn daughter, Chayla. To top it off, I was working crazy hours. Amid all of that, God was doing incredible things in our lives. Fan into Flame Ministries was born out of that crucible. The idea would grow and be tempered over the years by moments of Spirit-led engagement and by intense personal suffering. For Allana, these days bore the fruit of true beauty. For me, the focus became hupomone (because I am a geek, and Greek is cool), or patience, endurance, and perseverance. And still it continues to be at the core, the call to fan into flame that gift in ourselves and in others.

Let's backtrack a little.

> *Paul, an apostle of Christ Jesus by the will of God,
> according to the promise of life in Christ Jesus,*
>
> *To Timothy, my beloved son: Grace, mercy* and
> *peace from God the Father and Christ Jesus our
> Lord.*
>
> *I thank God, whom I serve with a clear conscience
> the way my forefathers did, as I constantly
> remember you in my prayers night and day, longing
> to see you, even as I recall your tears, so that I may
> be filled with joy. For I am mindful of the sincere
> faith within you, which first dwelt in your
> grandmother Lois and your mother Eunice, and I am
> sure that* it is *in you as well.*

—2 Tim. 1:1–5

Paul takes Timothy down memory lane for a minute. He
reminds him that he is Paul's son in the faith. Why does
Paul do this? He wants Timothy to remember an incredibly
special moment in his life, the moment he received Jesus
Christ as Lord and Savior, the moment God's gift was so
graciously bestowed on a young man. I must wonder if
Timothy did not tear up a little, thinking of his father in the
faith facing death in Rome. Perhaps he felt a little shame
that the difficulties of ministry in Ephesus had worn him
down. Yet Paul brushes all that away. Striking to the core of
hupomone and without using the word, Paul tells Timothy

to "fan into flame the gift of God" (2 Tim. 1:6 NIV). There is nothing else we can do to endure as children of God.

I have heard this verse taught as a call to utilize those very special and individual gifts that God has bestowed on each one of us. God does desire us to serve Him with all our gifts, but the context of the verses that follow make it clear that Paul is talking about one gift. I will capitalize it and designate it the Gift. The cool thing is that this Gift is the same one for all and yet manifests itself very differently in each of us.

> *For God has not given us a spirit of timidity, but of power and love and discipline.*

> —2 Tim. 1:7

There it is—the Gift. It is nothing less than God Himself given to each of us who believe and confess. It is this Gift that makes us bold, endowing us with power, love, and self-discipline. It is a special power available only through Jesus Christ. It is power not as the world gives or recognizes power. It is the power to testify of Jesus and to stand with our brothers and sisters in Christ. It is power that is inextricably joined to love, and power without love is vain and useless.

> *If I speak with the tongues of men and of angels, but do not have love, I have become a noisy gong or a clanging cymbal. If I have the gift of prophecy, and know all mysteries and all knowledge; and if I have*

108

*all faith, so as to remove mountains, but do not have
love, I am nothing.*

—1 Cor. 13:1–2

This Gift is one that empowers without limit, motivates in love, and operates with self-discipline even as Christ Himself cried out in Gethsemane, "My Father, if it is possible, let this cup pass from Me; yet not as I will, but as You will" (Matt. 26:39). In a moment that the whole world around Him saw as the greatest weakness, Jesus exploded the chains of sin and death with the greatest demonstration of power, motivated by love and operating in self-discipline as only God Himself could do.

> *Who has saved us and called us with a
> holy calling, not according to our works, but
> according to His own purpose and grace which was
> granted us in Christ Jesus from all eternity, but now
> has been revealed by the appearing of our
> Savior Christ Jesus, who abolished death and
> brought life and immortality to light through the
> gospel.*

—2 Tim. 1:9–10

HE HAS SAVED US! And He has called us by grace, a grace that is eternal. But He did not just call us to a holy life and leave us to our own pitiful attempts. He provided the Gift. It is the Gift of revealed grace. It is the Gift of revealed life eternal. It is the Gift of the truth, the Gift of the good news and great joy that shall be to all people. It is the Gift that endows us with the same power that confounded the Law and threw the world into confusion. How foolish would we be not to fan that Gift into flame in our lives?

Chapter 8

The Proving of a True Lover

My son, thou art not yet strong and prudent in thy love.

Wherefore, O my Lord?

Because for a little opposition thou fallest away from thy undertakings, and too eagerly seekest after consolation. The strong lover standeth fast in temptations, and believeth not the evil persuasions of the enemy. As in prosperity I please him, so in adversity I do not displease.

The prudent lover considerest not the gift of the lover so much as the love of the giver. He looketh for the affection more than the value, and setteth all gifts lower than the Beloved. The noble lover resteth not in the gift, but in Me above every gift.

—Thomas à Kempis, *The Imitation of Christ*

In the above passage from *The Imitation of Christ,* Thomas à Kempis in a dialogue with his Lord and Savior examines the quality of hupomone love. Though written in the fifteenth century, it stands as a challenging definition of love.

"Wherefore, O my Lord?" protests our protagonist. It is perhaps our arrogance in self-reflection that most aptly defines our lack of prudent love. We are like the unprepared virgins, not realizing our lack of oil until it is too late or until the Lord Himself calls us out and we stop our frantic efforts to listen carefully to His words. Kempis utilizes this conversation milieu throughout this work. It is more than a literary device. Kempis highlights the need for us to be in constant communication with God.

It is only when we accept conversation with Him as a lifestyle that we move forward in our imitation of Christ. This is more than Sunday mornings and perhaps Wednesday evenings. It is even more than daily devotions and scheduled times of prayer. These things are not bad, but perhaps consider them disciplines of faith as opposed to conversations of love. We often do them out of a sense of duty, not out of a heart of love. A discipline can become mechanical and void of meaning. A loving relationship and the conversations that must accompany it are filled with meaning and feed life into the disciplines. We are called to be in relationship with God 7 days a week, 24 hours a day. When we do that, we are well on our way to imitating Christ.

Hupomone love listens to the words of our Lord and recognizes the truth of His assessment. It is an everyday, every-hour, every-minute relationship.

Kempis says, "for a little opposition"—the Lord uncovers our instability in love. The word *circumstance* comes up again and again in our hupomone discussion. Whether it is our love for God or our love for those around us, when a little opposition raises its head, how quickly we fall away. When the sky is falling and disaster raises its ugly head, we tend to cling to our Lord and Savior and band together to battle the oncoming doom. It is the "little oppositions" that send us running, too often to places we should not go. We drop the armor of God for the tranquilizing pillows of consolation. When we take our eyes off of Jesus and begin to look at the circumstances of our lives as our guides, we forfeit the effectiveness of His promise to be with us always. Notice that I said "effectiveness." The promise stands, and the truth is eternal. It is when we flee in the face of the little things—the "little opposition"—that we crash and burn when the world throws its weight at us.

Hupomone love does not fall down or drop its armor at the first sign of trouble.

Strong

Kempis refers to "the strong lover"—the fodder of many a dime store novel. Yet too often the hero or heroine is just the opposite of Kempis' hero, plunging instead into temptation and believing the persuasion that the fulfillment of lust justifies any behavior. Jesus is our great example of love. He is the archetype of hupomone.

Have this attitude in yourselves which was also in Christ Jesus, who, although He existed in the form of God, did not regard equality with God a thing to be grasped, but emptied Himself, taking the form of a bond-servant, and *being made in the likeness of men. Being found in appearance as a man, He humbled Himself by becoming obedient to the point of death, even death on a cross.*

—Phil. 2:5–8

Christ stood fast. He stayed the course to complete a plan that called for the complete sacrifice and abasement of His very being. He rejected the lies of the enemy time after time. He rejected that Matthew could never be anything except a crooked tax collector. He rejected that a woman named Mary Magdalene was too soiled to be of any use to anyone. He rejected that a woman of Samaria could never serve the gospel. He rejected that humanity was not worth the sacrifice. He rejected that a young man who was raised in the faith but walked away wreaking destruction all around him for 25 years could not turn his life around and become a tool of the Holy Spirit and a man who sees value in imitating Christ.

But God demonstrates His own love toward us, in that while we were yet sinners, Christ died for us.

—Rom. 5:8

114

For God so loved the world, that He gave His only begotten Son, that whoever believes in Him shall not perish, but have eternal life.

—John 3:16

This is love. It stands fast in truth. The strong lover is based not on circumstances but on the gospel. It is a love that is truly for richer or poorer, in sickness and in health, but its strength transcends the grave.

> *For I am convinced that neither death, nor life, nor angels, nor principalities, nor things present, nor things to come, nor powers, nor height, nor depth, nor any other created thing, will be able to separate us from the love of God, which is in Christ Jesus our Lord.*

—Rom. 8:38–39

This is the love God has for us, and it is the love that is required of any who would be proved a true lover.

Prudent

> *prudent* (adjective)
> acting with or showing care and thought for the future

Kempis has uncovered the weak lover—the one who falls away in the storm, seeking only consolation. He has proclaimed the strong lover—the one who stands fast in the face of temptation and whose love does not rest on the whims of circumstance. Now we find that there is yet another quality of love we are called to in our imitation of Christ. The Lord turns His conversation to the prudent lover.

How often we mistake the gift for the lover. This is the sign of imprudent love. The gift is wonderful and amazing. We wrap ourselves up in the gift. We hug it and caress it. We proclaim the gift to the world. It thrills the soul, but like all gifts, it fades in value. The storms of life batter the gift, and the sands of time wear it down. Suddenly, that thrill is gone, that tingle that we called love has faded away. And because we have been so focused on the gift instead of the lover, prudent love that might have been is never found.

Jesus speaks of this love.

> *Others fell on the rocky places, where they did not have much soil; and immediately they sprang up, because they had no depth of soil. But when the sun had risen, they were scorched; and because they had no root, they withered away.*

> —Matt. 13:5–6

The gift of the gospel is heard and perhaps even believed, but the faith that springs up is in the gift, not in the giver, not in the lover of our souls. So when the circumstances of life arise, there is no depth to hold our faith because our eyes are not on Jesus.

> *Fixing our eyes on Jesus, the author and perfecter of faith, who for the joy set before Him endured the cross, despising the shame, and has sat down at the right hand of the throne of God.*

—Heb. 12:2

As great as the gift is ("For the wages of sin is death, but the free gift of God is eternal life in Christ Jesus our Lord" (Rom. 6:23)), it is only great because it opens the path for us to focus on the lover.

As is so often the case, the qualities of our vertical relationship with God speak into our horizontal relationships as well. The gifts of our life, both given and received, should be conduits of intimacy drawing us into relationships with others. When the gifts are the focus, the love is compromised, and when circumstances change, we find that it is not love at all. We are all too often ready to believe that gifts (given or received) are enough, but there is no endurance in gifts when they do not bring clarity of focus on the lover.

The prudent lover looks to the future, not to the present or the past. The actions of the prudent lover are framed to sustain and grow intimacy over time with the beloved. That is the focus of a steadfast relationship, one that will stand the test of time. It is that kind of love that Paul speaks about in 1 Corinthians.

> *Love is patient, love is kind and is not jealous; love does not brag and is not arrogant, does not act unbecomingly; it does not seek its own, is not provoked, does not take into account a wrong suffered, does not rejoice in unrighteousness, but rejoices with the truth; bears all things, believes all things, hopes all things, endures all things.*

—1 Cor. 13:4–8

Be prudent in love, setting *all* gifts lower in value than the lover who gives them.

The Noble Lover

no·ble (adjective)
1. belonging to a hereditary class with high social or political status; aristocratic.
synonyms: aristocratic, patrician, blue-blooded, high-born, titled; archaic: gentle
2. having or showing fine personal qualities or high moral principles and ideals.
synonyms: righteous, virtuous, good, honorable, upright, decent, worthy, moral, ethical, reputable

Strong, prudent, and noble—Kempis offers these as the attributes of someone who loves well, as spoken by God to someone who has not achieved the status of a strong and prudent lover. He defines the first two attributes in terms of action. The strong lover stands fast in the face of opposition. The prudent lover looks past the gifts and sees the value of the lover or beloved behind them. When I look at the noble lover, the definition is not in action but in position.

Kempis wrote *The Imitation of Christ* as a series of booklets in the early 1400s. The concept of nobility was much more defined and important then in the daily lives of almost everyone. It was widely believed that nobility was a matter of birth and that noble birth predicated a higher standard of behavior. In Christian nations, nobility was given a foundation in the will of God. History reveals the flaw in this thinking (stemming from the basic flaw in humanity— sin). Kempis himself was the son of a blacksmith and apparently entered monastic life due to the influence of his older brother. Still, this idea of noble—the idea of position—was a very real one to him and to the people who read his writings.

Kempis proposes a position in his description of the noble lover. It is a position of stillness. He originally wrote in Latin and used the word *quiescere* for stillness.

> *Nobilis amator non quiescit in dono, sed in me super omne donum.*

A Roman would have used the word *quiescere* to say good night (*bene valeas et quiecas*). God is calling us into a

119

position of rest in Him. Kempis recognizes that we tend to rest in the gifts or the positive circumstances we find ourselves in and not in being the lover who gives us these gifts. I find a cool parallel in the periodic table. The noble gases sit at one side of the table. They are called such because they are generally nonreactive to their environment. That quality in nitrogen is why it is used to preserve foods in sealed containers and used as a replacement for compressed air in filling tires. The nitrogen will not react to the food or to the rubber of the tires in the way oxygen does.

Our love for God should not be reactive to the things around us or the circumstances of our lives. It should rest in Him above all those things—*"in Me super omne donum."* Matthew records an exchange between Jesus and an "expert in the law."

> *"Teacher, which is the great commandment in the Law?" And He said to him, "'YOU SHALL LOVE THE LORD YOUR GOD WITH ALL YOUR HEART, AND WITH ALL YOUR SOUL, AND WITH ALL YOUR MIND.' This is the great and foremost commandment. The second is like it, 'YOU SHALL LOVE YOUR NEIGHBOR AS YOURSELF.' On these two commandments depend the whole Law and the Prophets."*
>
> —Matt. 22:36–40

The first and greatest commandment is to love God, and He sets the standard of that love.

But God demonstrates His own love toward us, in that while we were yet sinners, Christ died for us.

—Rom. 5:8

The flawless demonstrated His love for the flawed. It is not based on anything we have to give or offer.

For I am convinced that neither death nor life, neither angels nor demons, neither the present nor the future, nor any powers, neither height nor depth, nor anything else in all creation, will be able to separate us from the love of God that is in Christ Jesus our Lord.

—Rom. 8:38–39

The intrinsic focus of God's love begets its noble nature, completely unaffected by circumstance since God is completely unaffected by circumstance. That is both the great example of noble love and the measure of the noble lover. It is in this love that we find rest, not in the many gifts He gives but in who He is.

Chapter 9

Make It Personal

I have, to some degree, learned the tension of walking through the valley of the shadow of death while still expecting blessing. I can navigate suffering (relatively speaking) but expect blessing. So when I knew I was flying to Shanghai, I decided to be specific in my request to God. I bought a coach seat but wanted an upgrade. Not only did I want an upgrade, I wanted to be upgraded to the upper deck of the 747 aircraft in seat 77. When I checked my flight just before our Sunday gathering at the Bridge MetroWest, I saw I had been upgraded to seat 77. See, in the grand scheme of things it's a small thing. In light of recent events, it's insignificant. But it means something to me that the Father cares about the little things that seem big to His kids in the moment. That's what Dads do. He's a good, good Father.

—Social Media Post from My Brother

In the Details

I am not going to go into all the history and details of why I hold my brother in high regard as a Hupomone Man, but he has shown me that walking in the miraculous should be a way of life. It is a lifestyle that extends from our faith.

As my brother says, we have a "good, good Father," one who gives His children good gifts (Luke 11:13). The mistake we make too often is linking the gifts from our Father to the circumstances of our lives and our own expectations. When we become a new creation, we are freed from circumstances, and our only expectation is that "all things work together for good" (Rom. 8:28).

Our freedom and expectation of God's good makes the miraculous details of God's love all the more amazing, because whether you get upgraded to seat 77 or your flight is canceled and you are stuck in the airport for 36 hours, the goodness of our Father remains, along with the expectation of the miraculous. Joy is guaranteed. We just need to walk it out. This is not the giddy joy of circumstance; it is the hupomone joy. It is the joy that remains regardless of circumstance but brings those "oh yeah" moments when God opens the gates of heaven to bless in demonstrative fashion and strengthen the hupomone faith of creatures born of circumstance.

Being Home

> *Even the sparrow has found a home,*
>   *and the swallow a nest for herself,*
>   *where she may have her young—*
> *a place near your altar,*
>   LORD *Almighty, my King and my God.*

—Ps. 84:3

Turn right onto 140. Take a slight right onto Highland, and continue through the S curve onto North Vine Street. Turn left onto Reservoir Road, and then make a right onto Violet Circle. Going home really doesn't seem such a big deal to most of us. Simple directions like these bring us home—well, at least they bring us to a place where we have a roof over our heads.

"Honey when you are home, you are not really home." Allana's words stung. Of course, I was home. I knew my address and could navigate my way there. Her statement was so subtle and reached so deeply into who I was that it would not be until years later that I would see the truth in it. This particular disability strikes deeply, separating us from the hupomone God who loves us just as it separates us from those around us who would do the same. We cannot remain under or in a place we have never really been. As I look back, I can see God calling to me so many times, "Beloved, when you are home, you are not really home."

Walking through the motions of "getting home" does not cut it. There is an undeniably spiritual aspect of *home*. More importantly, it takes a spiritual intentionality to enter into a home relationship with anyone, but especially with God.

> *Then the Lord said,*
>
> *"Because this people draw near with their words*
> *And honor Me with their lip service,*
> *But they remove their hearts far from Me,*
> *And their reverence for Me consists of tradition*
> *learned* by rote."

—Isa. 29:13

The Israelites knew the way *home*. If you asked them, they would tell you they were home. They followed the traditions, they followed the Law, they sacrificed, they celebrated; they did all these things and believed it meant *home*. They were wrong, and there would be consequences just as there are for all of us.

> *Therefore behold, I will once again deal marvelously*
> *with this people, wondrously marvelous;*
> *And the wisdom of their wise men will perish,*
> *And the discernment of their discerning men will be*
> *concealed.*

—Isa. 29:14

I wish I could say that today I am an expert at being home, that it comes naturally. The truth is that old habits die hard, and the technologies of the twenty-first century makes it easier than ever to not be wherever you are. Being home requires an ongoing commitment to God, to my family, and to all the people God brings into my life.

Detour Ahead

Detour Ahead! How I have dreaded that sign. Fortunately, with today's smartphone and GPS technology, detours do not carry the same fear factor they did when I was younger. In fact, today with a little bit of effort, we are able to avoid detours altogether, and if we do get stuck in one, with a few simple screen touches we no longer have to rely on the often sparsely placed detour signs and can map out our new path to our destination. However, we have not managed a technology that will predict and map out alternative routes to our goals when we hit those life detours that take us away from the path of life we have planned.

> *de·tour* (noun)
> the act of going or traveling to a place along a way
> that is different from the usual or planned way
> a road or highway that you travel on when the usual
> way of traveling cannot be used

I really struggled with this topic for some time. I originally thought I would be talking about heavenly detours, how God diverts our path for His purpose, and we just have to kind of ride along. That is certainly how I felt about the things that were going on in my life. On January 2, 2013, Nisa Faith had just joined our family after a 10-year odyssey of losses, tears, and suffering. Allana was feeling a little ill, but we were certain a quick trip to the obstetrician and some antibiotics would make us good to go. What a difference three days can make. Three short days and I would be on perhaps the greatest detour of my life. Or would I?

God has been really battering me on this subject because I have truly felt that this was a detour when in reality it was right on course. But instead of my course or Allana's course, it is *God's* course. When we view these events in our lives as detours, we detract from God's omniscient role as master planner of everything. I want to step lightly here because I am not writing doctrine on God's sovereignty, nor am I suggesting that God gave this horrible disease to Allana or anyone else.

I think that perhaps my concept of our situation, whether thought out or not, was of God looking down and saying, "Oh shoot! Allana has leukemia. Well, I guess I can use that for My glory until we can get things back on course." There we go—just a heavenly detour, and I am so tempted to detour here into writing the very doctrinal statement that I said was not my intent. Thank God for the delete button. However, what I have found is that God does not take detours. Allana and I are not on some end around that will eventually get us back on the path that God has for us. We *are* on the path He has carefully laid out for us.

Now the word of the LORD came to me saying,

> *"Before I formed you in the womb I knew you,*
> *And before you were born I consecrated you;*
> *I have appointed you a prophet to the nations."*

—Jer. 1:4–5

No detours for God's consecrated, God's appointed, God's anointed. There is a point in every born-again believer's life that he or she makes a choice to change direction. However, this is not a detour because not only does the route change, the destination changes. The believer is no longer on a pathway to eternal separation from God, to hell, but has turned to a path leading to the mind of Christ. There is an intentional, continual seeking of God's presence. It harks more of the etymological root of the word than our current usage.

> French *détour*
> to divert, to turn

To turn from—this is the very heart of repentance and salvation. There is one major difference when we submit ourselves to our Lord and Savior Jesus Christ. There is not just a temporary course change; there is a change of destination, and I do not just mean heaven. Every person has in mind a course and a destination. What the destination will be is determined by our core values. Some pursue riches. Some pursue power. Some pursue pure evil. Some pursue the greatest good. And some pursue nothing

128

at all, seeking to have no destination but to simply see life as riding out each circumstance to the best of their ability, only to find that this is in itself pursuing a course to a destination. When one comes into a personal relationship with Jesus Christ, all of that changes.

> *And we know that God causes all things to work together for good to those who love God, to those who are called according to His purpose.*
> —Rom. 8:28

Suddenly, we are on a new course. It is not one of our own creation but one that God set into motion before the world was created. This is the confusion. We conceive of where God has us headed, and when things don't turn out, we see it as a detour. That brings frustration just the same way that an unexpected detour on the road unsettles us. However, when we give God the glory He is due, that evaporates. "The mind of man plans his way, but the LORD directs his steps" (Prov. 16:9). It is the assumption that God has it all under control that allows us to continually apply His Word to our situation. "I considered my ways and turned my feet to Your testimonies" (Ps. 119:59). It is in this place that God affirms us, even amid the storm.

Chapter 10

Hupomone Men

*I thank my God always, making mention of
you in my prayers, because I hear of your
love and of the faith which you have toward
the Lord Jesus and toward all the saints; and
I pray that the fellowship of your faith may
become effective through the knowledge of
every good thing which is in you for Christ's
sake. For I have come to have much joy and
comfort in your love, because the hearts of
the saints have been refreshed through you,
brother.*

—Philemon 1:4–7

Philemon—I must wonder if it is the least read of all the
books of the New Testament. It is unfortunate because it
contains one of the most beautiful stories of redemption
and reconciliation. The story centers on three men: Paul
the Apostle; Onesimus the slave; and Philemon, the leader
of a church that met in his home, which was typical of the
early church. He was also a slave owner and specifically
owned a slave named Onesimus.

Strangely enough, we are not going to focus on the theme
of the letter. Instead, we are going to take a quick look at

the man Philemon and the qualities that make him a Hupomone Man.

People Pray for Philemon

The Apostle Paul prays for Philemon. And if Paul remembered Philemon in his prayers, I am going to assume that others did also. A true Hupomone Man inspires prayer by the exemplary life he leads.

Paul's words are extremely specific here. "I always thank my God as I remember you." We might make the mistake of thinking that Paul is referring here to a prayer of thanksgiving for this wonderful man of God. There would be nothing wrong with that, but it is not what Paul is saying. He is praying for Philemon as he continues his hupomone ministry in Colossae.

The placement of this phrase, immediately following the greeting, speaks of the importance that he knows Philemon places on this subject. The Hupomone Man values prayer. He values a life of constant communication with God (1 Thess. 5:17), and in this particular case, he values the prayers of others on his behalf.

People Talk about the Hupomone Man

When people talk about the Hupomone Man, they do not talk about the amazing things he has accomplished. They do not talk about all the books he has written. They do not even talk about the incredible ministry he has built. "I hear of your love and of the faith which you have toward the Lord Jesus and toward all the saints" (Philem. 1:5). They talk about his love for people and his faith in Jesus. Don't get me wrong, all the Hupomone Men we have discussed were men of action, but it is the heart and soul that defines hupomone, not the results of that heart and soul.

He Is Willing to Collaborate

Partnership comes naturally to the Hupomone Man. *"And I pray* that the fellowship of your faith may become effective through the knowledge of every good thing which is in you for Christ's sake" (Philem. 1:6). The Holy Spirit cultivates collaboration among God's people, very often among people very dissimilar or with competing priorities. Consider the struggles of Paul and Barnabas and the motley crew of the 12 disciples. Jonathon's future clashed directly with the anointing of David. The spies at Jericho and Rahab had very little in common, but together they brought down a city and paved the way for the Messiah. These collaborations serve to deepen our understanding of the faith.

He Cultivates Joy and Encouragement

If the joy of the Lord is his strength, then the Hupomone Man likes to spread his strength around. "For I have come to have much joy and comfort in your love" (Philem. 1:7). It is the essence of the Holy Spirit flowing out of him and to those around him that extinguishes fear with encouragement. That is not tied to circumstances but to the source of all hupomone, God Himself.

He Refreshes

The word *refresh* that Paul uses is the same word Jesus used when He said, "Come to Me, all who are weary and heavy-laden, and I will give you rest" (Matt. 11:28). The Hupomone Man is quite simply allowing the very basic qualities of his Lord and Savior to flow out of him. He calls out to those around him to cease their futile labors. *Anapaow* is a form of the Greek word for *pause*. Literally it is an up-pause. The presence of a Hupomone Man brings an up-pause.

Paul gives us a snapshot of the Hupomone Man. It is a mirror for Philemon to look at as he stepped into a personal and cultural challenge. Onesimus, Philemon's slave and property had run away. Apparently, he had stolen from Philemon as well. Somehow, this runaway slave met with Paul in Rome. Onesimus became a brother in the faith and told Paul what had occurred. Paul sent Onesimus back to Philemon, instigating a journey in faith and hupomone living for both of them. Scripture leaves us to our own interpretation of the outcome of the journey, but church tradition tells us that some years later, Philemon and Onesimus were martyred side by side after proclaiming the gospel message and establishing them both as Hupomone Men.

Onesiphorus

> *The Lord grant mercy to the house of Onesiphorus,*
> *for he often refreshed me and was not ashamed of*
> *my chains; but when he was in Rome, he eagerly*
> *searched for me and found me—the Lord grant him*
> *to find mercy from the Lord on that day—and you*
> *know very well what services he rendered at*
> *Ephesus.*

—2 Tim. 1:16–18

Everything we know from the Bible about Onesiphorus is in 2 Timothy. That is significant because Paul knew his execution was near when he wrote this final epistle of encouragement to Timothy. Orthodox tradition tells us that Onesiphorus was one of the 70 disciples sent out by Jesus. These men were the second tier of intimates to Jesus after the 12. Roman Catholic and Orthodox tradition hold that Onesiphorus was martyred in a town called Parium not far from Ephesus where Timothy served God by leading the church in that pagan city.

While we do not have a lot of details, Paul tells us volumes about this man Onesiphorus. When I read about him, the picture of a Hupomone Man came into focus. Paul actually began this passage with comments about two men who were not Hupomone Men. When the going got tough in Rome, Phygelus and Hermogenes got going—out of Rome or at least away from Paul. Onesiphorus, on the other hand, eagerly searched for Paul, knowing the difficult circumstances Paul was in and the very real danger that association with Paul brought during this time. This is the nature of the Hupomone Man—steadfastness, constancy, and endurance. It is not swerving from your deliberate purpose and loyalty to faith and piety by even the greatest trials and sufferings.

Unfortunately, the concept has too often been hijacked to mean some kind of groaning endurance as we wait to be taken to heaven. This is not what we find in Onesiphorus. Let's walk backward through this brief exposition on a Hupomone Man.

1. Eager

The Hupomone Man is eager to serve. He understands the greatest commandments as Jesus taught them.

> *And He said to him, "'YOU SHALL LOVE THE LORD YOUR GOD WITH ALL YOUR HEART, AND WITH ALL YOUR SOUL, AND WITH ALL YOUR MIND.' This is the great and foremost commandment. The second is like it, 'YOU SHALL LOVE YOUR NEIGHBOR AS YOURSELF.' On these two commandments depend the whole Law and the Prophets."*

> —Matt. 22: 37–40

This makes him eager to serve and eager to follow the hand of God wherever it leads, whether into the streets of poverty, the halls of power, or simply to the side of a suffering fellow follower of Jesus. Perhaps it is with Onesiphorus in mind that Paul penned this description of love: "Love...does not act unbecomingly; it does not seek its own, is not provoked, does not take into account a wrong suffered" (1 Cor. 13:5). The eagerness of the Hupomone Man is not born of self-interest. Onesiphorus gained nothing by seeking out Paul. In fact, it may have begun the series of events that would lead to his martyrdom. What do we search for eagerly?

2. Unashamed

The Hupomone Man is unashamed of the truth that has been entrusted to God's people. Onesiphorus was unashamed of the gospel and not afraid of the chains and danger it brought. There is a certain pride that is the hallmark of the Hupomone Man. It is a pride born of the understanding of our position as children of God. It is a pride born of a 1 Corinthians 13 love and grounded in the Great Commandments. Paul raises up the relatively unknown man of God to Timothy, an example of the exhortation, "Therefore do not be ashamed of the testimony of our Lord or of me His prisoner, but join with *me* in suffering for the gospel according to the power of God" (2 Tim. 1:8).

3. Refreshing

The Hupomone Man is a breath of fresh air in a dank and dark room, a ray of light shining in the darkness. When someone perseveres through hard times in the abundance of Christ, there is an aura of refreshment that permeates the situation. What an amazing testament to this little-known man of God, for, as Paul said, "he often refreshed me" (2 Tim. 1:16). This is a quality that Onesiphorus brought to even the most difficult situations. It is the very nature of Jesus Christ shining through his children who are empowered by the Holy Spirit. "The thief comes only to steal and kill and destroy; I came that they might have life and have it abundantly" (John 10:10).

Paul ends this passage about Onesiphorus with "and you know very well what services he rendered at Ephesus" (2 Tim. 1:18). The Hupomone Man carries his qualities wherever he goes. It did not matter whether he was on the streets of Ephesus or in the halls of power in Rome comforting Paul as the specter of execution hovered nearby. Onesiphorus was eager to serve, unashamed of the gospel, and he brought refreshment to those around him.

Onesimus

I appeal to you for my child Onesimus, whom I have begotten in my imprisonment, who formerly was useless to you, but now is useful both to you and to me.

—Philem. 1:10–11

Onesimus was a slave. While not the lowest of the low in that society, he was pretty far down the list. Then he became a runaway slave and went even lower. We do not have the back story of Onesimus, but Paul probably did when he penned these words. However, the details do not really matter because at its core, this is the story of humanity. I love these verses because in an obscure book using what might seem purely concrete language, Paul summarizes the work of the Holy Spirit in our lives. The Holy Spirit takes what was formerly useless and makes it useful. It is Romans 8 in a nutshell.

> *For the mind set on the flesh is death, but the mind set on the Spirit is life and peace, because the mind set on the flesh is hostile toward God...and those who are in the flesh cannot please God.*

> —Rom. 8:6–8

Paul makes it clear that the change from useless to useful is not about the performance of duties. It is also not about a change in life status. Paul acknowledges that Onesimus is Philemon's property. There is no impassioned plea to free the slaves. How often we want to link our progress from useless to useful on a change in circumstances. The lie of Satan is that our usefulness rests in circumstances. Yet Paul begs Philemon to recognize the work of the Holy Spirit in Onesimus' life, transforming him from a useless slave to much more—a beloved brother, "no longer as a slave, but more than a slave, a beloved brother, especially to me, but how much more to you, both in the flesh and in the Lord" (Philem. 1:16).

Paul then does something amazing, which serves as an example to us all. He engages the transformation from useless to useful on a personal level. He leverages his own reputation and his own usefulness to aver the spiritual change in Onesimus and to square the life debt he incurred. The model is inescapable, demonstrating the way Jesus stands before the throne and answers the accusations of the devil. "But if he has wronged you in any way or owes you anything, charge that to my account" (Philem. 1:18). What a wonderful illustration of our Lord and Savior's advocacy for us! It is also a wonderful illustration of the way we should be standing in the gap for our brothers and sisters in Christ. Just as Jesus stands with us and offers Himself to erase the debt of our sin, we should stand ready to leverage ourselves in the service of those to whom the Holy Spirit leads us as we serve Him.

While the Bible does not give us the rest of the story, church tradition tells us that some years later, Philemon and Onesimus were martyred for their faith—together.

Chapter 11

Hupomone Re-viewed

Behold, I will do something new,
Now it will spring forth;
Will you not be aware of it?
I will even make a roadway in the wilderness,
Rivers in the desert.

Isa. 43:19

Living the hupomone lifestyle does not just happen. It is a process because it is intertwined with relationship. It is the living out of 2 Corinthians 5:17: "Therefore if anyone is in Christ, *he is* a new creature; the old things passed away; behold, new things have come." We enter into relationship with God, and He engages a process in us that moves us deeper into Him and the truth He holds. It is a process of redefining everything we know to be true.

After Allana was diagnosed with leukemia, our lives were a madhouse. People asked the question, and I found myself saying over and over, "We have had to redefine what a good day is and what a bad day is." The new normal for Allana, me, and our family was a bad day by the old standards—every day. As I thought about this redefining process and my relationship to God, it became clear to me that my relationship with God is the catalyst and the key to that process. That is what God does for us. That is how He grows us and draws us close.

A burning bush redefined life for Moses. Suddenly, a good day was risking his life standing before Pharaoh or before his very own irate people. I cannot help but wonder if Moses did not wish for the good old days of tending sheep in the hills of Midian. Joseph had his days redefined in Egypt several times. An angel by a wine press redefined a good day for Gideon. Job—well, Job is Job, and he is perhaps the poster child for the redefining process. Jesus redefined a good day for the disciples over and over and over. Then He redefined it for the universe by dying on Calvary. I can almost hear God that day in his best Jerry Maguire impression speaking something like this to His people, "You know our little venture? Well it had a big day, a really big day. Now I complete you!"

Each of these examples has a real element of *bad* to them. It is important to realize that God does not want us to suffer, but He *uses* it and, yes, *allows* it because it serves His purposes in achieving Romans 8:28, which outlines the result of the redefining process. The good thing about this process is that it has a core. It is a core that is made of rock-hard, incorruptible, absolute truth. It is a core that is omnipresent, omniscient, omnipotent, and immutable.

This redefinition process is different for everyone. It does not take cancer, captivity, or persecution to dive into relationship with God. The hupomone principle can reach into your life right where you are and by the power of the

Holy Spirit redefine everything so you can participate in godly perseverance.

What happens is that in all this redefinition, we come to a single truth.

> *He has told you, O man, what is good;*
> *And what does the* LORD *require of you*
> *But to do justice, and to love kindness,*
> *And to walk humbly with your God?*

—Micah 6:8

Circumstances change, but a good day is when we do justice, love kindness, and walk humbly with our God. I cannot say that today was a good day, but I believe and I am learning that God gives grace and power to make tomorrow a good day, no matter the circumstances.

Made in the USA
Middletown, DE
05 August 2022